W9-COU-931

for *Women*
Over
50

PUBLISHED BY

BOSTON AMERICA CORP.

www.bostonamerica.com

125 WALNUT STREET, WATERTOWN, MASSACHUSETTS 02472

TEL: (617) 923 1111 • FAX: (617) 923 8839

KAVET'S INTERNET SITES FOR WOMEN OVER 50: ISBN 1-889647-57-8. PRINTED IN U.S.A.

Written by Karen C. Kavet

Designed by Victoria Bocash of *Inktree Design*

Some General Women's Sites

www.shesgotittogether.com
A general site for women with everything from cuisine to business.

www.ivillage.com
Another everything site covering a woman's world from astrology to working from home.

www.bbb.org
This is the home of the Better Business Bureau and if you want to turn in any scoundrels they tell you how to do it.

www.womenshealth.com
A broad site with lots of information. PMS hotline, health library, online Rx refills, great links and women's health news.

www.nytimes.com/specials/women/ whome/index.html
This site is so comprehensive and has so much information that you hardly need to ever go anywhere else. Enter here only if you have the whole afternoon.

www.awomansguide.com
Its goal is to provide factual nutritional and medical information to women but it seems to be a load of miscellaneous links and a push to sell vitamins.

Want to get started fast? You don't even have to bother reading my introduction. Here are some sites that have almost everything. Don't just jot them down and then not buy the book.

Introduction

Reaching 50 is a wonderful milestone. My God, it's half a century. Think of all the wisdom, knowledge and experience we've picked up in that time. And the wrinkles. Being 50 sometimes feels as if we are entering the invisible period of our lives. People turn their heads when we enter a room and then, likely as not cause we're not young and sexy, tend to dismiss us. The book will give you the places to find the information on health, fitness, financial security, education, menopause and all the things that affect you, and this information may inspire you with new ideas for enriching your life.

Apology and Disclaimer

When I wrote this book all the sites listed were live and available. When you go to some of them you'll find they've disappeared. God only knows where they go. Some will disappear and some will come back an hour later and some will somehow evolve into a site for Korean folk remedies translated into Hungarian. The internet is indeed a mysterious place. My best advice, if this happens, is to simply move on to the next site. There are plenty listed in each category and the ones that are anxious to sell you something will probably be available longer than some teenager's homesite or looney trying to cure indigestion with grass seeds.

Lots of people are trying to get rich using the internet, me included, and many of the sites listed here are commercial enterprises trying to suck you into $29.95 a month. If these people are successful I suppose their sites will be around for a long while. I've tried to find mostly free sites but these also tend to disappear when the host gets bored with working for nothing. Regardless, while you can find all these sites for yourself (especially if your time is worth 9 cents an hour) I've done lots of the leg work and locating just one or two useful sites will be easily worth more than the ridiculously low price of this book.

That said, the author, publisher and distributors of this book cannot take responsibility for what you find or don't find or what these sites lead you to, even the pornographic stuff that I didn't intend, or what you may buy and then get stuck with or any of the fascinating, frustrating and endless paths of the internet. Hey, it's the internet. What do you want me to do.

How to Use Your Computer

In case you got a new computer along with this book you may need some instruction on how to use it. If you have kids, get one of them to hook it up and teach you how to get online. If you never bothered to have kids, don't worry. First of all everyone has some geeky friend who knows all about computers and will be thrilled if you ask them to help. Let these people set up everything so all you have to do is click on a little icon and information pops up. Whatever you do don't open the instructions that came with the computer or use the HELP menu and try to do it yourself. Not only will this frustrate you but it also voids your warranty.

Once you get online have your friend show you where all the chat sites are with the sexy guys - no I'm kidding - ask him where the little box is where you type in the www stuff. Then type in the line of gibberish and a notice will appear that this site can't be found. There will be a bunch of suggestions on what to do but none of them will work so just go onto another site.

Women's Health

You know the old saying. "If you have your health you have everything". You really believe this when you're 50 and your back starts going out, you can't sleep soundly and your stomach is so uncooperative that you swallow antacid pills like M&M's. This section will give you information on your aging body and suggestions for keeping it young. They do work. I'm 50 and my kids think I'm only 28.

Women's Medical

Okay, we're not invincible anymore. We go for an annual physical and watch our diet and trying on bathing suits has become a chore. We're sore for 3 days after gardening or cleaning out the attic. We find our stomachs are suddenly very choosy about what they will accept, our hair is turning gray and just maybe, thinning a little. It's time to start learning something about what makes our bodies tick and what we can expect from them. These sites will do that.

www.coloradohealthnet.org
Harder than usual to find the right info, but worth the effort. Point to Site Overview and then click on Women's Center. The Mayo Clinic's Health Center with information on cancer, fitness and appearance, gynecologic conditions, medical tests and procedures, menopause, osteoporosis, prevention and wellness.

www.allhealth.com/womens
Covers most women's health concerns through links to articles by professionals.

bewell.healthgate.com/womenshealth/index.asp
General women's health site, including subjects of interest to mature women. That's us.

content.health.msn.com/focus_topic/her
This women's health resource will answer your questions on emotional wellness, nutrition, illnesses, sexuality, drugs and other subjects.

www.womens-health.org
The Society for Women's Health Research tries to rectify biases in medical research and has comprehensive links to every problem you hope you'll never have.

www.womens-health.com
An excellent interactive learning environment that facilitates the exchange of information. Headaches, midlife health, mental health, menstrual problems, health news and lots more.

- **www.planetrx.com**

  This company sells all the health products you find in a drug store and also provides information on various health questions.

- **www.womenshealth.org**

  This forum goes into every aspect of women's health, breaking it down into sections on sex, gyn, body, mind, looks, food and many more categories.

- **www.4woman.org**

  The National Women's Health Information Center provides a gateway to a vast array of Federal and other women's health information. It's run by your government and they wouldn't lie.

- **www.ourbodiesourselves.org**

  Excerpts and information from the classic women's book "Our Bodies, Our Selves". After reading this you'll want to buy the latest edition.

- **www.wellweb.com/WOMEN/WOMEN.HTM**

  Detailed information on every problem you pray you'll never have and the ability to chat with other patients about it.

I don't want you to think I'm a hypochondriac or anything. I am including all these medical sites because, if you're like me, your doctor is too busy to take the time to fully explain them in the few minutes your health plan allows them to spend with you. Should you become an activist and get the doctor to explain everything, your health insurance rates will likely double.

Aging

We're not there yet but if you like to worry this page will give you the gory and glorious details on women aging. If you prefer you could also just rip this page out and plan to peruse it in 10 years or so.

www.aarp.org/programs/women/home.html
Women in their midlife are likely to suffer from more illness and discrimination than their male counterparts. This site tells you where to get help if the guys are pushing you around.

www.nhlbi.nih.gov/whi/index.html
The Women's Health Initiative gives you all the places that are studying subjects of concern to women such as hormone replacement or calcium supplementation. You can get the latest information from these research locations.

www.nih.gov/niams/news/calsum.htm
This study gives you the absolute final word on optimum calcium intake.

www.ninds.nih.gov/patients/Disorder/ALZHEIMR/alzheimers.htm
If you can type in this address and still remember what you are looking for you don't have Alzheimer's.

www.nih.gov/nia/health/pubpub/pubpub.htm
A good site run by the National Institute On Aging that gives information on everything you may be worried about from constipation to health quackery.

Plastic Surgery

www.surgery.org/procedures/home.html
Introduction to cosmetic (only) surgical procedures from the American Society of Aesthetic Plastic Surgery. Detailed information on each type of plastic surgery and a searchable list of surgeons certified by the American Board of Plastic Surgeons.

www.plasticsurgery.org/surgery/prcdidx.htm
Web Site sponsored by the American Society of Plastic Surgeons and the Plastic Surgery Educational Foundation offering links to all types of reconstructive and cosmetic surgery. You can also find a list of surgeons in your area.

www.surgery.com
Provides information about cosmetic surgery procedures. Assists in locating a surgeon, reviewing the surgeon's credentials, viewing before and after photographs of the surgeon's work and even e-mailing the surgeon directly. You pick the area you would like to improve, and before and after pictures provide a realistic view of the actual improvement. Links to Plastic Surgeons in your area.

www.onlinesurgery.com/live/index.html
If you have Real Player, you can watch, on-line, any number of plastic surgical procedures. Choose from face lift, liposuction, breast reduction or enhancement, nose job. See post-op interviews. Not for the faint of heart.

www.plasticsurgery.org/surgery/dermabra.htm
Refinishing the skin, also known as dermabrasion and dermaplaning gives the skin a smoother appearance. It is most often used to smooth out facial wrinkles, treat deep acne scars, or remove pre-cancerous growths.

Let's face it, we've been thinking about this for years and we know so many women who have had cosmetic surgery to correct those wrinkles, sagging thighs or drooping breasts. It's a little frightening, and perhaps more so after you read about what they are actually going to do with knives but the results are tempting. Learn more about it here before you even talk to a doctor.

Back Pain

Does your back "go out" more than you do? Do you have your chiropractor's number on your speed dial? I do and you might as well garner all the information you can on your back because it's the weak link in our bodies ever since we decided to walk upright and have sex in the missionary position. If you can manage to use your computer while lying on your back with your knees bent it may help.

www.ninds.nih.gov/patients/Disorder/back%20pain/backpain.htm
The National Institute of Health will tell you all about back pain. It probably won't help.

www.ama-assn.org/insight/spec_con/patient/pat007.htm
The AMA tells you everything about prevention and treatment of back pain.

www.aaos.org/wordhtml/pat_educ.htm
Orthopaedic surgeons tell you about your back as well as the rest of your bones and muscles and problems from shoes to carpel tunnel.

www.vh.org/Patients/IHB/Ortho/BackPatient/Contents.html
This site is published by a non-government panel of experts and has excellent and sound advice on back pain and prevention.

www.mayohealth.org/mayo/9402/htm/backcare.htm
The Mayo clinic gives you all they know about back pain. Short of seeing an expert in person this is sound stuff.

Menopause

- **www.hoptechno.com/book38.htm**
  Basic information on menopause presented by Hopkins Technology.

- **cpmcnet.columbia.edu/texts/guide/ hmg09_0010.html#top**
  Another basic site of information on menopause, its symptoms and treatments.

- **www.menopause-online.com**
  Provides women with up-to-date, easy to use information. Contains sections devoted to treatments, herbal remedies, vitamins, and an interactive bulletin board.

- **www.pslgroup.com/MENOPAUSE.HTM**
  An information-filled site with links to medical news and alerts, menopause information, newsgroups and discussion groups.

- **www.fbhc.org/Patients/BetterHealth/Menopause**
  Developed by the Foundation for Better Health Care, this site presents an introduction to menopause, information on estrogen and progesterone, health changes after menopause, symptoms, FAQ's, and links to other related sites.

It's coming and it doesn't go away; the hot sweats and all the decisions on hormones. Speaking of estrogen, the data changes each month about the side and long term effects so don't let this week's articles scare you too much.

Menopause

> Hot flashes are the biggest subject of conversation among my friends and let me tell you, male doctors don't really understand, and it's not in your mind and I guess I feel it deserves another page.

www.plannedparenthood.org/ WOMENSHEALTH/menopause.htm

Planned Parenthood's totally upbeat site on menopause. It'll make you glad you've finally reached this time in your life.

www.aoa.dhhs.gov/aoa/pages/agepages/ hormone.html

From the Administration on Aging, information dedicated to "Hormone Replacement Therapy - Should you Take It?"

www.power-surge.com

Great graphics, music and upbeat home page of Power Surge. This site gives you a warm and caring community for women at midlife.

www.mothernature.com/ency/ Concern/Menopause.asp

MotherNature.com's site for alternative approaches to menopause.

alt.support.menopause

A great support site and resource-base for women going through 'the silent passage'. Medical, social, physical, sexual, and relationship issues are the most popular topics of discussion.

Breast Cancer

- **www.msnbc.com/news/BRCANCER_Front.asp**
  The latest studies, tests, trends, and prevention.

- **www.fight-breastcancer.com**
  A highly regarded breast cancer resource with survivor stories, myths, state initiatives and a reminder that nothing replaces early detection.

- **www2.cancer.org/bcn/index.html**
  The American Cancer Society's breast cancer network with survivorship, information, resources and news.

- **www.acor.org**
  A free online cancer information site with excellent links to new developments and a very encouraging reconstruction story.

- **www.cancerhelp.com/ed**
  Frequently asked questions on coping with and surviving breast cancer from Edu-Care's breast cancer network.

- **www.graylab.ac.uk/cancernet/600062.html**
  National Cancer Institute's site on Inflammatory Breast Cancer.

- **www.breastcancerinfo.com**
  This breast cancer foundation brings you the latest developments and very moving survivor stories.

Here lies our greatest fear and it's important to learn all you can because, other than not smoking, early detection is the best defense you have. Should you be frightened by a scary report you can read about all the women that won their battle.

Sexually Transmitted Diseases

At your age you should know better but in the event there are some funny rashes itching around your body this is the place to find out just what you may have caught. Dealing with how you got it is another matter entirely.

www.mdchoice.com/Pt/PtInfo/std.asp
A brief explanation of various sexually transmitted diseases. The search boxes at the top of the site will give you more information than you want.

www.mediconsult.com
A comprehensive site that gives you information on everything that can go wrong. Just pick a condition that is troubling you and let the doctors fill you with fear.

www.condomania.com
Avoid trouble next time with one of this company's many styles of condoms. They even rate different brands.

www.healthanswers.com
Just click on STD and receive expert advice on so many scary diseases that you'll learn to keep your knees together.

www.healthlinkusa.com/276feat.htm
A very comprehensive site with a wide range of information and links to even more.

Vision Concerns

•••⦂ **ophthalmology.about.com**
   An excellent overview on all the new eye surgery techniques. Search under "vision correction" on the bottom and you'll learn enough to get your Ophthalmologist degree.

•••⦂ **www.asklasikdocs.com**
   Board certified surgeons answer every possible question on Lasik surgery in great detail.

•••⦂ **www.lasersite.com**
   Laser eye surgery explained and a directory of doctors who perform this surgery.

•••⦂ **www.ftc.gov/bcp/conline/pubs/health/vision.htm**
   This government site has an excellent discussion of vision correction procedures. It really helps you to read between the lines of all the different options available to you.

•••⦂ **www.aoa.dhhs.gov/aoa/pages/agepages/eyes.html**
   Aging and your eyes. Your government gives you the honest poop.

Can't see as well at night? Sick of your contact lenses or glasses? Been hearing about the new surgical vision correcting procedures? I for one have been interested for years but I've been a coward when it comes to sharp objects or lasers fooling with my eyes. In case you are braver, here is the place to learn more.

Weight Stuff and Nutrition

It's normal to gain a little weight as you grow older but there comes a time when you have to draw the line in the sand or end up wearing full figured sizes. These sites will help you at least establish some bench marks about where you should be and what you should be eating to get there.

www.americanheart.org/Whats_News/ AHA_News_Releases/obesitytips.html
Tips on finding a healthy weight for yourself from the American Heart Association. By the time, of course, that you've correctly typed in this address you'll have lost a pound or two.

www.eatright.org/nfs/nfs51.html
American Dietetic Assoc. answers questions on nutrition and fitness.

www.thriveonline.com/health/Library/ CAD/abstract1638.html
Fitness, nutrition, sexuality and serenity. What more do you need?

www.fitnessmagazine.com
Mind, body and spirit for women from Fitness Magazine. Lots of good articles.

www.acsh.org/nutrition/index.html
The American Council on Fitness and Health will give you articles on every food that will cure or kill you.

12653

Gary - 7-11-58

Mike - 2-20-61

Dave - 5-13-

Me - 8-1-50

Nutrition

- **www.ama-assn.org/insight/spec_con/patient/pat070.htm**

  Why you should eat more fruits and vegetables. You've heard all this before and still you go for the jelly donuts.

- **www.4woman.gov/bodyimage/index.htm**

  The Department of Health and Human Services has this well-done site on women's body image and health. All the exercise and nutrition information that you've been ignoring.

- **www.cdc.gov/nccdphp/sgr/sgr.htm**

  This is the Surgeon General's report on the relationship between physical activity and health. You've got to believe it.

- **www.niddk.nih.gov/health/nutrit/nutrit.htm**

  I don't want to say too much but this is the site for people with real disorders like binge eating and obesity. Check it out in the privacy of your home.

- **www.nlm.nih.gov/medlineplus/eatingdisorders.html**

  More on eating disorders. I really hope you don't need this page.

You've been hearing this your whole life and you've even tried to bend your family's eating habits to match the latest theories. Now it's time to make the final resolutions, learn the "food pyramid" and cut out the heavy cream, butter and lamb chops. There really is no alternative. Either you listen to these ridiculously skinny nutritionists or you get some horrible disease.

Fitness

More exercise. That's the one thing all the magazines insist will extend your life and you never see an article disputing it 6 months later. So get with it and I hope you'll find a little inspiration from some of these sites.

- **www.fitnesslink.com**
  A neat site with all sorts of information on exercise, nutrition and gyms.

- **www.acefitness.org**
  This site lists 40,000 certified personal trainers. One of them has to be cute and live close enough to be able to teach you.

- **www.primusweb.com/fitnesspartner/ library/libindex.htm**
  Excellent equipment and book reviews. Check this out before you spend money.

- **www.pitt.edu/~pahnet**
  The Physical Activity and Health network tells you how beneficial exercise is, with basic articles from the leading sources. You've probably heard all this before but now you're old enough to listen.

- **www.ama-assn.org/insight/gen_hlth/fitness/ fitness.htm**
  The AMA gives you all the good reasons to exercise and a basic fitness program.

Diets

www.catabolic.com

This diet claims to work 3 times faster than starvation. It's based on 100 foods that burn more calories, being digested, than they provide. It costs $19.95 to learn what they are.

www.dietinfo.com/diets.htm

This site lists a zillion diets, clinics and centers. If you follow each for a day you'll end up weighing nothing.

www.dietsite.com

A free service that will analyze your diet. They also talk about sport nutrition and alternative nutrition which seems to mean herbs.

www.obesity.com

A scary web address, Obesity.com (Da-da-da-dum), but there is very well-presented information on health and weight loss and yes, a number to tell you if you are obese.

There are millions, maybe billions of diets on the web and in fact anytime your computer is working too slowly you can be sure it's because fat people are looking up more diets. Now I know my readers aren't "fat" but perhaps would only like to lose a few pounds. You will find some great and some very funny diets here and one is bound to work.

Diets

Some of the diet sites on these pages offer serious help. Others offer ridiculous fantasy. Now that you're over 50 I assume you'll be able to pick out the difference and I'm including the ridiculous ones for your amusement.

www.cambridgediet.com
With the Cambridge diet you buy and eat a lot of their goo and they promise you'll lose weight.

www.weightwatchers.com
Weight Watchers must work cause they have meetings all over the world. They offered to find one in your country and I picked a place named EESTI, God only knows where, and sure enough they had a Weight Watchers. What's more the site was in EESTIAN or whatever.

www.prevention.com/weight/wlwb
You just tell them what you'd like to weigh and they'll tell you just how many calories a day you can eat. The 71 weight loss tips are pretty good.

www.nutra-slim.com/mega4.html
This site is a scream. The special Accelerated Fat Burning diet lets you "burn up fat" even while you sleep. Mostly you'll just keep clicking on wild claims until you reach the $19.95 plus $4.85 shipping and handling finale.

www.oxycise.com
With this weight loss program you don't diet or take pills or buy gadgets. You just use oxygen. All you have to do is buy the videos, and breathe, and you'll be skinny in no time.

The Stuff You Eat and What It Does To You

www.navigator.tufts.edu

This site performs a remarkable service in rating over 200 nutritional web sites based on accuracy, depth of information and usability.

www.mayohealth.org

The Mayo Clinic's Health Oasis has a nutrition center that Tufts rated the highest. You might as well get your nutritional information from the best.

www.pueblo.gsa.gov

According to the Tufts rating your government is on the stick here with an excellent site that gives good information on food and its effect on your health.

vm.cfsan.fda.gov/list.html

A complex and serious site but if you have a particular subject in mind here is where you get the real poop. Look up, for example, Health Claims On Food.

www.ama-assn.org/consumer.htm

The AMA Health Insight is a very useable site with excellent information on everything you should or shouldn't stick in your stomach. You have to believe them, they're your doctors.

www.cyberdiet.com

A fun site with all the tools you need to plan a healthful diet. Check out the "Fast Food Quest" and see what you are really eating.

When you get to be 50 you can no longer eat and drink with abandon. You start to carry antacid pills everywhere and no longer sleep well if you eat onions, garlic or cream pies after 9 PM. These sites will give you some idea of what's good for you and not, if you haven't already figured it out.

Hair Thinning and Loss Problems

More women than you'd imagine find their hair thinning as they get older. Most of the research, of course, has gone towards helping men but in the last few years some studies are starting to address women's concerns.

www.regrowth.com
A very comprehensive site with all sorts of treatments and remedies from green tea to transplants and an honest evaluation of each.

hometown.aol.com/hairbook/index.htm
Hair Loss Information Center gives a superb background on hair and its characteristics and a detailed analysis of each kind of treatment.

www.ahlc.org
The American Hair Loss Council's non-profit site that facilitates the exchange of information about hair loss. Loads of sound information.

www.pslgroup.com/HAIRLOSS.HTM
Doctors' guide to hair loss. A good discussion.

www.hairsource.com
This site sells all sorts of non-prescription hair loss remedies. You're 50. I assume you can figure out the scams.

S kin

www.cdc.gov/chooseyourcover
You may still love the sun but after reading this you'll learn to cover up and use lots of sun block.

www.aad.org/patient_intro.html
Dermatologists will frighten you even more about skin cancer but also give you information on varicose veins and acne (You don't still have acne?).

www.mayohealth.org/mayo/library/htm/tocskinc.htm
You can hardly find a better source of advice on every kind of skin condition than this site from the Mayo Clinic.

www.nlm.nih.gov/medlineplus/skinhairandnails.html
This long site is your government giving you the honest facts on skin, hair and nails. You won't find anti-aging creams and magic bust enlargers here.

www.nytimes.com/specials/women/warchive/960619_1213.html
Amongst much other information this site will convince you to stop smoking. It seems it causes wrinkles.

All those days at the beach have taken their toll. Why didn't they tell us how dangerous the sun was 35 years ago? As if we'd have listened. My own kids still insist on frying themselves. There is some hope. After reading the mostly warnings on these sites check out the plastic surgery which, if you have the courage and cash, can remedy almost anything.

Alcohol

Alcohol can be a real health problem. Too much that is. A little is supposed to be good, at least this month. Mostly the people who are having trouble with their drinking won't admit it so this page probably will do little good but.... perhaps you have a friend.

content.health.msn.com/content/article/1674.50182
Information when alcohol becomes a problem.

www.alcoholics-anonymous.org
If you have friends who needs help Alcoholics-Anonymous is the place to send them.

www.ncadd.org
The National Council on Alcohol and Drug Dependence. Don't let the picture of the founder scare you. There is good information here.

alcoholism.miningco.com/health/alcoholism
Links to a billion (well maybe a hundred) alcohol-problem related areas.

www.health.org
A real lot of information from the National Clearinghouse for Alcohol and Drug Information. If you read all of this you'll have no time left to drink.

Alternative Medicine

homeopathic-md-do.com
This is a national list of real MD's who practice classical homeopathy which as I understand it consists of giving you an extremely diluted form of a poison in an appropriate dose matched to the poison that is making you sick. Or something like that.

www.powerfate.com
This product, for only $39.95, claims to actually makes good luck happen. It works by absorbing all the "negatives" in your life. In case it doesn't work there is a PowerEnhancer for only an additional $9. And a money back guarantee no less. Don't miss this site if you need good luck.

spiritualnetwork.com/links/New
You can click on this site for actual divine insights ($70 per hour) and links to such diverse "medical treatments" as Hemp Oil, Tarot readings, Shazam Astrology, Aumara Light and Healing circles and other things that defy human comprehension.

www.lisco.com/wuebben/TM/health.html
Maharishi Vedic creates heaven on earth with this website of bliss and enlightenment.

If you hate to go to doctors or if you don't trust doctors or if the doctors haven't been able to cure what ails you there is always alternative medicine to turn to. With alternative medicine you can often get totally untrained quacks and dangerous unsanitary nuts to do ridiculous things to your body. The funny thing is sometimes these treatments work. Who am I to knock them. Some kinds of alternative medicine have even entered mainstream health care. So here are some places where you can read about alternative treatments and make your own judgments.

Memory

At 50 you haven't lost it yet but you are starting to see the signs of forgetfulness. "Now, where did I put those car keys", and "what did I go into the garage for" and "her name is on the tip of my tongue". So here are some sites to help cope with the problem before you become a babbling idiot and can't find the way to the toilet.

- **www.epub.org.br/cm/n01/memo/memory.htm**
  The mechanisms of memory, the loss of memory and how to improve your memory. There are two important ways. One is to relax. I forget the other.

- **piebald.princeton.edu/mb427/1997/students/learning/people.html**
  A concise introduction to human memory. Like, if, for example, you can remember this site's address.

- **www.exploratorium.edu/memory/dont_forget**
  Games and activities to test your memory and techniques to help you improve it.

- **www.memoryzine.com**
  You can purchase a course on CD's to help improve your memory.

- **www.markgiles.co.uk/methods.html**
  Secrets that magicians use and you can learn to improve your memory. They include rhyming, familiar links and other methods that are all nicely explained.

Sleeping and Snoring Problems

www.sleep-sdca.com
This sleep disorder site sure lists a load of sleeping problems. It's enough to make you loose sleep. Take the self test. You'll probably fall asleep before you reach question 30.

www.newtechpub.com/phantom
Let Phantom Sleep Resources (there's a name that inspires confidence) handle your sleep problems. Find out if you have Apnea, whatever that is, and try not to lose sleep worrying about it.

www.supertips.com/fw/1067.htm
For only $6.95 they'll sell you a book with 67 good ways to sleep. Me? I just stick a pillow over my head.

www.nshsleep.com/test.cfm
Take this test from Northside Hospital's Sleep Medicine Institute and send it to them. You'll get feedback on your responses. Ask for a second opinion.

www.snoring-strips.com
This site sells "chin up breathing strips" which you stick around his jaw and hope no one sees him because he'll look pretty ridiculous. They swear it helps.

www.snoringless.com
For 20 bucks you spray this stuff in his throat and it lubricates the snoring spot so everything is quiet.

hometown.aol.com/roctex69/myhomepage/index.html
Here's a good solution. This site sells some sort of electronic earplug that you wear and they swear you can't hear a thing.

If you're like me you no longer can sleep till noon what with the hot flashes and all. In fact, you have trouble sleeping through the night and getting up to pee every now and then is starting to appear a very necessary thing to do. Well these sites just might give you some ideas on how sleep works and how to handle snoring problems so perhaps you can "sleep like a baby" again.

29

Dental Concerns

People sometimes call this the gold and silver age of our lives. Unfortunately much of this gold and silver is in our teeth. We've learned not to bite down too hard on pretzels and not to open tough pistachio nuts with our teeth. Though I debated putting such a terrifying subject in the book I'm spending more and more time with dentists and it seems worthwhile to know something about the subject. Besides, I'm having some transplants done and maybe the dentist will give me a break if I pitch the profession.

www.dental-implants.com

If you are going to have an implant it's a good idea to read this page and learn something about the procedure. The cost can range from $500 to $6,000 per implant so at least look around a little to try to find the $500 kind that don't rust.

www.dentistinfo.com

Find a dentist, lists of dental terms but best of all frequently asked questions like "what exactly is a root canal" but you really don't want to know.

www.dentistdirectory.com

You can get email answers to all your dental questions here for free. It's a lot better than going to have your mouth violated. But in case that doesn't stop the problem there is also a directory of dentists.

www.toothinfo.com

This is a great public service site with no sponsors. The Dental Consumer Advisor gives lots of health facts about dentistry, great diagrams and even an article on "How Honest Are Dentists".

www.dentalfear.org

If you're scared to death of dentists this is the site you need. It deals with dental phobia and how you can handle it short of flossing after each meal so you never have to go to the dentist.

www.smilevision.com

If you are unhappy with your smile, these days it's a cinch to fix it.

Mental Health

www.mentalhelp.net
An award winning online guide to mental health and psychiatry. They even have a mental health store with herbs and stuff to make you better.

www.metanoia.org/choose/index.html
Sound advice on choosing a mental help therapist in case life just doesn't seem to be working or you are hurting inside.

depression.about.com/health/depression
An extensive guide to depression and information on causes, defining it, treatment, and much more.

www.mentalhealth.com
An encyclopedia of mental health information. The most common disorders are listed with description, diagnosis and treatment. Enough links to absolutely everything about the subject to truly drive you crazy.

www.mhsource.com/expert
This professor of psychiatry at Tufts provides a free service that will answer your e-mail questions.

These are the sites that will let you know if indeed your family is driving you crazy. I've found that by the time you're 50, however crazy or not you may be, you're pretty satisfied with your personality and not too interested in changing it. Perhaps you can use these sites to prove to yourself just how nutty everyone else is.

Recurring Dreams

Do you still have that dream about final exams? You know the one where you have to pass this course to graduate and you haven't been to a single class all year. A version that I sometimes have is being unable to find the exam room. Well, join the club and learn about other people who suffer the same way and maybe even learn what to do about it.

••••• **redrival.com/nightmare/dictionary.html**
Your online dream dictionary can help you remember and explain your dreams, if you dare. Most unpleasant dreams seem to have a basis in insecurity.

••••• **dreams.nsm.it/dreams/varie/bears.html**
Tell this site about your dreams and they will try to interpret them. I'm not so sure I'd want them to.

••••• **www.shpm.com/articles/dreams/index.shtml**
Self Help and Psychology magazine has some wonderful articles on using dreams to improve your life.

••••• **1st-spot.freeservers.com/topic_dreams.html**
A great list of sites about dreams. If you start checking these out you'll have no time left for sleeping.

••••• **www.lifetreks.com**
These people do research into dreams and need your dreams. You can give at the office (if you nap there) and also at home. Fun lists of other people's dreams.

Indigestion

- **www.naturalhealthconsult.com/ulcers.html**
  A good discussion of indigestion and a whole list of natural and medical products to treat the problem.

- **www.egregore.com/herb/Indigestion.htm**
  A guide to about 50 medicinal herbs and which will help your stomach problems.

- **4indigestion.4anything.com**
  A large resource with alternative medicine answers to your stomach problems but also doctor links.

- **www.1001herbs.com/menus/Poor_Digestion.html**
  A long, long list of herbs to treat indigestion. If you tried all of these you'd weigh 400 lbs.

- **www.mothernature.com/ency/Concern/Indigestion.asp**
  Mother Nature will give you all the good advice you need as only she can. This site has a nice balance of conventional and alternative treatments.

By the time you're 50 you understand just which foods are incompatible with your gastrointestinal system. Still if you really love those onions or peppers or salami or beans the occasional discomfort may be worth the taste especially if there is something you can take for it.

Sexuality

Sex has been there all our lives and sometimes I regret it took us so long to be allowed to enjoy it. From a subject that was only whispered about in our youth you can now get instructions on prime time TV. These sites will give you more detailed instruction and answer all the questions about which you have no one to talk to.

neuro-www.mgh.harvard.edu/forum_2/EpilepsyF/sexdrive.html
The Department of Neurology at Mass. General Hospital maintains this forum on sex drive and they should know what they're talking about.

gynpages.com
Abortion Clinics online. Just in case etc.

femina.cybergrrl.com/explorer.htm
Sites for, by and about women. You can learn all about subjects with which you are too embarrassed to talk to your best friends.

www.atfloydian.u-net.com/alt-contraceptives/home.htm
An amazingly comprehensive privately run site with information on alternative contraceptives as well as sterilization, sexual health and myths like avoiding pregnancy by jumping up and down after sex.

www.askisadora.com/index2.html
A sexuality forum that will keep you too busy with the discussions and links to even think of having sex.

www.sexologist.org
The American Board of Sexology. It seems they actually certify people to be sex therapists. If you need one check their credentials.

www.playcouples.com
Don't open this one unless you are very liberal minded.

www.todayswoman.com
This is supposed to be a general women's site with fashions and parenting and such but it seems to be mostly sex so we'll put it here.

Yoga

www.yogasite.com
An eclectic collection of yoga connections. It gives the postures and describes a dozen styles that will confuse you no end.

www.yogaclass.com
A lovely site with a free online yoga class. Here is an easy way to get started with no cost or embarrassment.

www.will-harris.com/yoga
Yoga exercises you can do at your desk. You'll feel great but your co-workers will think you've lost your marbles.

www.santosha.com/asanas/asana.html
Instructions on a long list of yoga poses. Pronouncing the names looks as difficult as bending 50 year old bodies into the positions.

www.sivananda.org
This award winning site has 345 pages. I wish reading them would only make you more flexible.

At 50 I'm finding my flexibility is starting to go and I was never flexible enough to afford to lose any. Women I know who are into yoga can not only bend themselves into pretzels but they all seem to have this happy relaxed attitude about life. There must be something to it.

Travel Information

Look, you're 50. If you don't see the world now just when are you going to do it? The time to take all those trips you've been dreaming about is while you have your health, sanity, vision and the ability to really enjoy them. This section has a bunch of pages that make travel planning and travel arrangements easy.

Women's Travel

• **womenstravelclub.com**
  Designed for women by women. They travel to over 20 destinations annually.

• **www.women-traveling.com**
  Women Traveling Together (WTT) offers escorted, all-inclusive tours for women of all ages who want the companionship and security a small group offers, while having the option to participate in planned activities or strike out on their own.

• **travellady.com/special.html**
  From Travellady Magazine, links to every special interest you could imagine (Adult travel, Animal Watch, Cooking Schools, Learning Vacations, you name it). Full descriptions and pictures of what you will see and do along with links to make your travel arrangements.

• **maiden-voyages.com/directory/ventures.html**
  Links to companies offering a broad range of trips including adventure, hiking/biking, dude ranches, cultural/theater, culinary. For the woman who is single or whose partner does not have the "travel bug."

• **www.rainbowadventures.com**
  Adventure travel for women over 30. We just make it.

Women traveling by themselves or with other women have different concerns and needs and an entire industry has grown up to meet them. Either that or they've realized we have lots of disposable income of our own and they want to get a share. The next few pages will put you in touch with these people.

Women's Travel

I must admit a group of women traveling on their own often evolves into a stress free noncompetitive vacation that eclipses anything you can experience with men around. Forget about feeling embarrassed. Leave the guys at home and find a new travel delight.

www.exploretravel.com/Women.html
Outdoor and cultural travel for women over 40.

www.expogardentours.com
Group tours to Europe, China, Costa Rica, New Zealand revolving around visits to renowned gardens.

www.womantours.com
Personalized, inn to inn road bike tours for women only. Designed to ensure unique opportunities for touring, adventure, and camaraderie for women of varied backgrounds, lifestyles, ages and cycling experiences.

www.travel-library.com/rtw/html/rtwwomen.html
Tips for women traveling in Asia and a good list of travel books for women.

www.tips4trips.com
A thousand pretty good travel tips for women and travelers in general.

On Line Travel Magazines for Women

- **www.passionfruit.com**
  A women's travel journal with thoughtful comments on foreign culture and peoples.

- **www.journeywoman.com**
  An online travel resource just for women.

- **maiden-voyages.com**
  An online edition of a women's travel magazine that lists lots of companies specializing in women's travel.

- **www.napanet.net/~satchel**
  A new travel magazine for women over 40.

- **www.pathfinder.com/travel/TL/tarticles/1132.html**
  Fifty tips for women traveling alone. They are quite simple but also very sound.

- **www.womenstravelclub.com/tips.html#street**
  Excellent safety and packing tips.

- **www.teleport.com/~earthwyz/women.htm**
  Earth friendly travels for women in a safe supportive environment.

Can you believe how specialized the world has become? Travel magazines just for women. They are finally realizing who controls the purse strings of the world. These magazines are a good continual source of travel ideas and information and the tips are particularly valuable.

irline Sites

To make reservations, find out schedules and most important get the extra frequent flier miles, book your flight on these sites.

Aloha Airlines	www.alohaair.com
Alaska Airlines	www.alaskaair.com
American Airlines	www.AA.com
American West Airlines	www.americawest.com
Continental Airlines	www.continental.com
Delta Airlines	www.delta-air.com
Northwest Airlines	www.nwa.com
Southwest Airlines	www.southwest.com
TransWorld Airline	www.twa.com
United Airlines	www.ual.com
US Airways	www.usairways.com

Some Foreign Airlines

Air Canada	www.aircanada.ca
Air France	www.airfrance.com
British Airways	www.british-airways.com
KLM Airlines	www.klm.com
Lufthansa	www.lufthansa.com
Swissair	www.swissair.com

Travel Books Online

- www.fodors.com

- www.frommers.com

- www.lonelyplanet.com

- travel.roughguides.com

- www.wtgonline.com/navigate/world.asp

- www.zagat.com

While these sites don't always give you the entire book (let them make a living) you can get an incredible amount of information about virtually every tourist location in the world. It is the smart place to look when you start planning a trip.

Worldwide Health Warnings and Information

If you're going to take a great vacation or trip the last thing you want is to die from some horrible disease that creeps up from your bare feet and infects your brain with a worm that exits through your nose or worse. Likewise most folk would rather not be kidnapped by mustached banditos who cut off ears for ransom. Check out these warning sites before making your non-refundable reservations.

www.who.int/emc/outbreak_news
Find out about the black plague before you leave.

www.cdc.gov/travel
Health requirements and medication recommendations for anywhere in the world.

travel.state.gov/travel_warnings.html
Travel warnings that even the CIA listens to.

www.tripprep.com/index.html
General trip information, health precautions, disease risk summary, official health data, and US advisories.

www.pathfinder.com/travel/TL/links/health.html
Links to multiple health sites. Everything from diving medicine to high altitude sickness.

Travel Clothing

•••⋮ www.exofficio.com
The ultimate clothing to see the world in. Clothing sorted by traveling needs such as evening out, stay warm, stay dry, in transit, active, urban.

•••⋮ www.tilley.com
This Canadian company sells top quality clothes and has some fun customs you're supposed to carry out when you meet someone else wearing their stuff.

•••⋮ www.travelsmith.com
I have personally used this company a great deal and have never been sorry.

•••⋮ www.fibronet.com.tw/wool/finepacking.html
This site tells you how to pack. It's pretty basic stuff but in case you haven't traveled since your honeymoon it might be a good review.

•••⋮ www.llbean.com
L.L. Bean where not only can you get travel clothes but also the pack to stuff them in.

You don't want to look like a frump when you are representing your country overseas, do you? Better get some of these wrinkle resistant, washable wonders from companies that specialize in travel wear. These clothes will also help you blend in with all the other tourists so the natives won't mistake you for someone with whom their family has a blood feud.

Active Vacations for 50 Year Olds

You've been to Europe, seen the States, recognize the hazards of too much sun on a beach and gained weight on cruises. Perhaps now you're ready for active vacations. These will take you to more remote places and teach you new things that you need to stay alive like Eskimo rolling your kayak, boiling your water and shaking deadly insects out of your boots. Should you make it home in one piece you'll need a week in bed before going back to work.

- **www.gorp.com/akdisc.htm**
  Alaska adventure trips. White water rafting, hiking, canoeing etc.

- **www.belize.com/reef%2Dscuba.html**
  Scuba diving and snorkeling in Belize on their barrier reef.

- **www.goski.com**
  Your ski vacation site.

- **courseguide.golfweb.com**
  This is a good guide to golf courses around the world.

- **www.greatoutdoors.com/index.html**
  Great outdoor activities of all kinds with links to equipment and ratings.

- **www.away.com**
  A travel company that specializes in adventure travel.

Active Vacations for 50 Year Olds

- **www.serendipityadventures.com/rugged.htm**
  Rafting, hiking, climbing, biking and more in Costa Rica.

- **www.fodors.com/sports**
  Over 500 sport and adventure trips in North America from sky diving to covered wagon trips.

- **www.llamatours.com**
  Llama tours in British Columbia.

- **www.beachs%2Dmca.com**
  Spend your vacation seeing the world from the back of a motorcycle.

- **www.outsidemag.com**
  Outside Magazine's site with destinations for active trips around the world.

- **www.spectrav.com**
  Adventure and special interest travel links to the operators of everything from dog sleds to cattle drives.

- **activetravel.about.com**
  A network of sites about all sorts of active trips plus every other kind.

On many of these trips you'll be mixing with people much younger than you are. This is a great way to keep thinking and acting young. Just bring along plenty of Advil® and you'll be fine.

Exotic Vacation Travel

If you are not going to wildly exotic spots at age 50, when will you be able to? After retirement, you say. By then your back or knees will be acting up and you won't enjoy yourself. 50 is a fine time to start seeing all those places you've been dreaming about and here are a few sites to whet your appetite.

www.aandktours.com/html/index.html
Abercrombie and Kent's site. Check out the Marco Polo Club for remote and exotic locations.

www.lonelyplanet.com/dest/dest.htm
Lonely Planet's in-depth descriptions of exotic locations.

www.hotwired.com/rough
This is the Rough Guide's site which gives information on exotic locations (14,000 they claim) around the world. The information is very detailed and complete.

www.africaarchipelago.com/home.html
This London agency specializes in travel to East Africa.

www.tourism-asia.com
The insider's guide to travel throughout Asia.

www.virtualnorth.net
Just type in the kind of arctic vacation you want and they will come up with the outfitters.

Financial and Legal Sites

You're 50. It's time to think about finances, retirement, managing your resources more seriously and perhaps even new careers. These sites can open up a vast exciting world of money management, entrepreneurship and give you all the tools such as law and insurance to guide you along.

Employment

If you are working you are probably the most valuable person in the company and your position is probably secure as all get up and these sites are included only to show you how easy it is to get a job nowadays so you'll feel even more secure. Should you be looking for a job or thinking of returning to the workplace you will find a whole new world of job hunting. If you have specialized skills or just general experience, and by the time you're 50 you have to have experience, it's likely someone is looking for you. With the internet's help it's become easy to find these companies.

www.suite101.com/welcome.cfm/ 50_issues_and_employment
Even though there are real scary articles on finding jobs after age 50 it's a superb site for employment.

content.careers.msn.com/gh.cfm
Good hints on resumes, interviews and negotiating offers. You'll feel so confident reading this you'll look forward to quitting.

midcareer.monster.com
A monster employment site that lists hundreds of thousands of jobs. Somebody out there must be looking for you.

www.careermosaic.com
You can post a resume here or search under whatever criteria you wish.

www.careerweb.com
Good career guidance plus the usual resume and job searches.

Social Security Information

- **www.ssa.gov**
  This government site is a little overpowering with all its information but is a good place to start checking to be sure they have records of all your money.

- **www.ssa.gov/about.htm**
  All the Social Security Administration's literature on retirement and things. It's fun to start planning.

- **www.ssa.gov/mystatement**
  Request a statement and check if those guys in Washington have had their greedy fingers in your account.

- **www.ssas.com**
  The Social Security Advisory Service provides non-governmental help to claimants, provides links and answers questions.

- **www.cpsr.org/cpsr/privacy/ssn/ssn.faq.html**
  Answers to interesting questions about Social Security.

Remember all those payroll taxes you've been paying all those years? Well they start coming back in about 15 years. Make sure some computer glitch didn't mess up your records and start planning what you'll do with all that Social Security money.

Stocks and Investments

With the vast amount of financial information on the internet every 50 year old dodo can have the tools to make intelligent investment decisions provided she makes the effort to study and understand. These sites will give you enough information to make reasonable investment decisions. Remember, however, you are competing against professionals who spend all day analyzing this information in addition to a network of buddies providing illegal inside intelligence. Should you get any of these tips yourself be sure to phone me.

moneycentral.msn.com/investor/research/welcome.asp
Money Central's stock research tool with lots of information on just about every company that's traded.

www.nyse.com
New York Stock Exchange quotes, listings and links to the listed companies.

www.nasdaq.com
All the information for stocks, indexes and companies listed on the NASDAQ.

www.cnbc.com
Business information, stock reports, a ticker search engine and financial data.

www.bigcharts.com
Charts of all the companies plus interactive charts to help you make your investment decisions.

www.cfol.com
This is the world's largest business and financial search engine.

www.financialweb.com
If you can absorb as much financial information as this site offers, you must be in the investment business already.

www.fool.com/radio/radio.htm
The Motley Fool takes an unconventional approach to investing, and going against the conventional thinking is often the smartest way to invest. I like this site.

Mutual Funds

- **www.standardandpoors.com/onfunds**
  Standard & Poor's Select Funds is an exclusive designation that indicates a fund has passed rigorous standards for continuity of performance and management.

- **www.fundalarm.com**
  This free site rings the alarm when managers change or funds change ownership. It's good stuff to know.

- **www.fundsinteractive.com**
  The web's top-rated fund site with everything from fund basics to news to profiles of managers. Links to 120 mutual fund groups.

- **www.fundz.com**
  The top 10 load and non load funds, all the major ratings of funds performance, research, top 40 fund internet sites and such.

- **members.aol.com/plweiss1/mfunds.htm**
  Mutual Funds made simple. Practical guidance on investing money, terminology, questions and answers and other information for beginning and intermediate investors.

- **www.mfea.com**
  The mutual fund investor's center with lots of information on mutual funds and 100 definitions that you'd better learn before you start to seek your fortune.

> These sites will give you a good overlook of mutual funds, their performance, who is running them, their focus and fees. As long as these fees are very low this is usually safer than trying to pick stocks on your own.

Law

If you have ever been involved in a legal dispute you know how expensive lawyers can be. It is often even more expensive to think you are a lawyer and try to do it yourself. Actually you can't win and that is why everyone feels the way they do about lawyers and there are so many "lawyer" jokes.

www.vix.com/pub/men/harass/harass.html
Sexual harassment law in case some pig is bugging you at work.

www.lawyers.com/lawyers-com/content/hiring/hiring.html
Good tips on hiring a lawyer and even advice on what it will cost.

www.abanet.org/referral/home.html
If you need a lawyer the American Bar Assoc. will give you the names of a few million.

freeadvice.com
This site offers answers to about 3,000 legal questions but if you have a good personal injury case they'll probably be at your door before you can turn your computer off.

www.lawyers.com/lawyers-com/executable/ask
Some very good answers to legal questions. At least one good lawyer dedicated his or her time to this site.

www.law.cornell.edu

If you are really ready to be your own lawyer this site gives you good pointers with constitutions, codes, court opinions and even ethics.

www.divorcenet.com

While I hope you will never need it, this site gives you a state by state breakdown of divorce law with lots of information on mothers' and even grandmothers' rights and everything else.

www.legaldocs.com

Write your own wills and leases. Save money and only get into trouble later (just kidding). Some forms are free and others from $3.50 to $27.75.

www.lawresearch.com

The Internet Law Library. This is the real McCoy and you can reference from 20,000 to 200,000 resource links should you happen to have time this afternoon.

www.catalaw.com

The catalog of catalogs of worldwide law on the internet. From aboriginal to women and gender law.

Practicing law by yourself can be dangerous but running to your lawyer for every decision will bankrupt you. The best approach is to have one of your kids go to law school and advise you for free.

Entrepreneurship

Now that the kids are older and you realize how soon they'll be gone it might be time to think about starting that little business in your garage. Most become worth billions in a few short years especially if you give them a high tech sounding name.

www.liraz.com

You can take a test and see if you have what it takes to be an entrepreneur, though it's pretty simplistic. They also sell entrepreneurial books and CD Roms.

entrepreneurs.about.com/smallbusiness/entrepreneurs

Lots of basics and good tips. Start reading this stuff before quitting your job.

www.entrepreneurmag.com

This online magazine has so many articles on starting and running your own business that you'll have to quit your regular job just to read them all.

www.score.org

This organization works in conjunction with the Small Business Administration and provides free advice to small companies from retired executives.

www.sba.gov/sbdc

Your government's Small Business Administration will give you money and advice and tips and brochures and counseling. Well, maybe they won't give you money.

www.businessnet.freeservers.com

"Free" advice for starting an online business so you too can go public and be a billionaire.

Women in Business

- **www.onlinewbc.org**
  Learn about entrepreneurship and business, running your own business, exchanging information and online business help from the Small Business Association.

- **www.bizresource.com**
  Support and information for small business owners and aspiring entrepreneurs. Newsletters, advice and tips.

- **www.e-magnify.com**
  Integrates education, business and career resources for women. Good basic advice on starting, expanding and leveraging your business.

- **www.bizplan.com**
  Help on creating a business plan with all the do's and don'ts.

- **www.womenconnect.com**
  Connecting women in business. A lot of good information on starting your own business.

- **www.bizwomen.com**
  Find business opportunities and develop networks and alliances with other women.

Women have been forming networks and supporting each other in business ventures for as long as men have thought they were the only ones who could earn a living. Some of these sites will enable you to learn from other women and develop contacts.

Taxes and Planning Advice

If the IRS audits your return just tell them you got all your information from their site on the internet. They'll never figure out just where you were and what you found and they'll let you off scott free. Don't call me.

www.nysscpa.org/sound_advice/sound_advice.html
Weekly financial advice from CPA's.

www.financenter.com
All sorts of calculators for helping make decisions on buying a car, saving for college, budgeting, insurance and other things involving your money. A very helpful site.

www.cnnfn.com
A very complete financial site that gives you all the tools you'll need for planning.

www.irs.gov
This site is run by the U.S. Treasury and they'd like to advise you to pay your taxes. I suppose they have interesting and useful information here but I just kept getting funny numbers.

www.irs.com
This commercial tax site is, at least, user friendly. They provide useful links, forms and software; some free, some cost.

I nsurance

www.insweb.com

This is a free service that lets you compare insurance quotes for leading companies to help you find the best rates.

www.farmersinsurance.com/fi3000.html

Farmers Insurance Company says they'll tell you all about insurance and I figured a farmer wouldn't lie so this is probably a good place to get information.

www.insure.com

More information about insurance than you are going to want. I think it's easier to listen to the insurance agent and get your free calendar.

www.insuremarket.com

You can get quotes online which should be useful for comparing with the prices you're now paying.

www.insweb.com

Insurance coverage and prices are a confusing subject so I guess it pays to get some free education and quotes to compare from sites like this.

Insurance is a mystery business if there ever was one. These sites help take some of the bewilderment out of the field and if nothing more you can easily get some comparative quotes without being pressured by still another insurance agent.

Food and Drink

By the time you're 50 you probably have established some strong preferences in what you eat and drink and have become a bit of an expert in your favorite wines or beer or Chinese food. Deciding what to have for dinner however, is a never ending problem with family preferences and favorites conflicting with nutrition and imaginative new tastes. Maybe you'll get lucky in this section and find some new dinners that everybody likes.

Food Magazines

- **www.pathfinder.com/FoodWine**
  The online edition of Food and Wine with cooking, entertainment, Epicurean lifestyle, home decorating and wine reviews.

- **www.epicurious.com/b_ba/b00_home/ba.html**
  Bon Appetit's online version with recipes and techniques, beer and wine, restaurants and stuff. You can type in a search of whatever you find in your refrigerator and come up with great recipes.

- **www.gourmet.com**
  Tap into Gourmet Magazine's data base and you'll be eating imaginative new meals for the rest of your life.

- **www.cookinglight.com**
  Cooking Light Magazine will give you some healthy alternatives for all the weight you've been putting on with the other magazine recipes.

- **www.vrg.org/journal**
  Fabulous archives from the Vegetarian Journal with recipes that will keep you happily eating forever.

Tired of the same old dinners? There are probably more recipes on the internet than overweight people at a state fair. Enjoy and indulge by surfing through various gourmet magazines and you'll soon discover sites with favorites that will enhance your eating pleasure and may even help your antacid problem.

Cooking

Your kids are probably out gomping on pizza and since you likely don't have to take them to McDonalds anymore you're left with more opportunities to indulge your pallet. There are endless sophisticated tastes waiting to find you and with a few clicks on these sites you can hook up with them.

www.geocities.com/NapaValley/4079/index.html
The list of almost 20 online cooking magazines alone will keep you busy for the rest of your life. The history and legends of foods is fascinating and then there are the recipes.

www.escoffier.com
This is a site for professional chefs but it has a great section telling you how to become one.

www.inquisitivecook.com
A super data base of answers to questions about cooking.

www.hoptechno.com/book1.htm
Dietary guidelines for Americans and splendid tips for healthy food preparation.

www.foodsubs.com
The Cook's Thesaurus with substitutions for thousands of ingredients. You can, for example, substitute Gow Choy for Ku Chai or Garlic Chives. Now I never knew that.

Recipes

...∴ www.epicurious.com

Features recipes from Bon Appetit and Gourmet Magazines. Data base of more than 10,000 recipes, searchable by keyword. Topical articles and guides to restaurants, cooking tools, seasonal cooking, and international eating.

...∴ www.allrecipes.com

Recipes by category, subdivided into additional categories (such as soups, vegetarian). Some recipes are rated. Recipe exchange.

...∴ food.homearts.com/food

Part of Women.com's network, just choose from type of dish, ingredients, cuisine, how many calories, complexity of recipe and time to prepare, and the perfect recipes will be displayed. You can even get a recipe by just telling them what you have on hand in your refrigerator.

...∴ www.geocities.com/Tokyo/Market/7773

Asian Recipe, where you can browse through numerous Asian cuisines, from Malaysan hot curry to delicate sushi.

...∴ www.foodsales.com/recipe.html

Recipes in many categories.

You're trying to come up with creative and healthy new dinners but you still have the cookbooks you got at your bridal shower. Perhaps the answer is in some really new modern recipes and if you spend a few hours on these sites you will be able to have a new dish every night.

Special Recipes

Vegetarians aren't the lunatic fringe they were when we were young. They're us. Everyone I know claims to "hardly ever" eat meat. Every time the experts study some grass eater in a third world country it seems they find some terrible disease that they seem immune to that is killing all of us. We don't, of course, starve to death at the same rate as these "healthy" aborigines.

www.fatfree.com
3,766 low-fat, vegetarian recipes to choose from. Also features discussions, USDA nutrient database, a list of vegetarian restaurants world-wide, and much more.

www.vegweb.com
Vegetarian and vegan recipes, chat, veggie info, questions and answers, and a link to Amazon.com books. Even explains what TVP is.

www.webvalue.net/recipes
Mouth watering vegetarian recipes like Mandarin Noodles and Stir Fried Spinach and Tofu.

www.recipecenter.com
More than 100,000 great vegetarian recipes. Recipe satisfaction guaranteed.

members.tripod.com/~peoplesreview/recipemovie.html
Each Thursday they post a new recipe and new movie suggestion.

www.planetveggie.com/bin/veggie.pl?item=1220-8
Vegetarian recipes for every course and every ingredient.

idt.net/~wordup/bread.html
This archive was started with the notion that although it is impossible to break bread with all the peoples of the world, at least we can share some recipes. Includes traditional recipes, bread machine recipes, and bread baking resources.

Foreign Food Recipes

● ● ● ● **soar.berkeley.edu/recipes/ethnic/chinese**
Over 800 Chinese food recipes. Who knew bird nest soup had a real bird nest in it.

● ● ● ● **library.thinkquest.org/10320/Recipes.htm**
Good "soul food" recipes and an interesting article on how they came about.

● ● ● ● **www.shango.net/cyberbride/sh.htm**
Secret Russian recipes along with some sort of music which I guess could be Russian. It drives you crazy after awhile.

● ● ● ● **www.sas.upenn.edu/African_Studies/ Cookbook/Ethiopia.html**
Not only Ethiopian recipes but an article on how their meal is served.

● ● ● ● **www.al-bab.com/maroc/food/food.htm**
Moroccan recipes enable you to enjoy some of the world's greatest cuisine.

● ● ● ● **www.latinsynergy.org/tm6.htm**
A really large number of Latin American recipes sorted by countries and links to even more.

● ● ● ● **soar.berkeley.edu/recipes/ethnic/indonesian**
A total of 113 Indonesian recipes and I hope you read the section on indigestion first.

In our neighborhood a new Thai restaurant opens every 15 seconds and it's not so hard to find Afghanistan or Ethiopian food either. Foreign foods open up a whole new world of eating and it's mostly lots healthier than our fat laden diet.

Gourmet Food Shopping

More fun than your regular market, these sites are not only an easy way to shop but expose you to unusual and special products and tastes and you had better be able to notice the difference because they're usually several times the cost of similar items at your super-market.

www.balducci.com/home.asp
Fancy and gourmet everything. You'll go broke just getting through the spice section. Much more fun than your regular supermarket.

www.onlygourmet.com
I had trouble just getting past the chocolate section.

www.bighornbuffalo.com
You can eat Buffalo meat just like the Indians did. It has a lot less fat than beef which is why you never see a fat Indian in movies.

www.glutenfreemall.com
This site has combined the catalogs of many dietary food manufacturers to bring you 880 gluten free products.

www.shoppinghunt.com/sallycat.asp?CatID=300
Sally has links to every specialty food item you'll want and some you won't.

www.bestcoffeebymail.com
They claim the best coffee and tea from around the world.

www.greatcoffee.com
Great coffees from around the world with ratings and descriptions of each along with coffee making equipment.

www.agrotrade.com
A fascinating place to shop for spices from around the world as well as tea, dried fruit and candies.

www.cornwellcoffee.com
Fresh Kona coffee direct from Hawaii. It sounds delicious.

Spices and Sauces

● ● ● **www.mustardstore.com/default.htm**
This is the world's biggest mustard store. If you tried to taste them all you'd burn your stomach out. There must be thousands.

● ● ● **www.chiletoday.com**
Every kind of Chili and salsa along with recipes, tips and hot tamale news.

● ● ● **emall.com/spice**
All the flavor secrets and spices of the orient. You'll never order take out Chinese food again.

● ● ● **www.americanspice.com**
Over 4,000 spices, oils, hot blends and other specialty supplies. If you can't find it here you don't want to put it in your stomach.

● ● ● **www.hothothot.com/hhh/index.shtml**
The hottest of the hot including tastes like "Sure Death", "Cyanide" and "D.O.A."

● ● ● **www.thewrath.com**
Hot sauces and salsa from "Religious Experience" along with some entertaining recipes.

More places to find the endless specialties and varieties that make cooking and eating such fun. The mustards alone would fill every cabinet I have in my kitchen.

F un Foods

Once I realized there were sites on bagels and pickles and garlic I just had to include them. God only knows what you are going to do with this page.

4bagels.4anything.com
What is a bagel and what is its history. This site has this kind of interesting information along with shops and franchises should you want to go into the business.

www.gourmetgarlicgardens.com
How to grow garlic, its health benefits, all the varieties and probably vastly more than you'd ever want to know about garlic.

www.matkurja.com/slo/country/food/gobe
How to find and prepare wild mushrooms without dying, which seems a goodly thing to learn.

www.dzpickles.com
Make your own pickles and sauerkraut with the kits this company sells.

www.fritolay.com/pretzel.html
The history and story of the pretzel.

Chocolate

www.hersheys.com/cookbook/chocolate/ideas
Lots of chocolate recipe ideas. If you open this site your diet is going to go to hell.

www.globalgourmet.com/food/ilc
Global Gourmet's I Love Chocolate site with mouth watering finds and recipes for each month as well as an archive that'll keep you well supplied with chocolate ideas.

www.godiva.com/recipes/terms.asp
A good glossary of chocolate and baking terms as well as tips and more dessert and chocolate recipes than you could consume in a lifetime.

productopia.austin360.com/ P/12/0,2557,12-451-0,FF.html
Life is too short to eat bad chocolate. This excellent site will teach you what to look for and give you buying advice.

www.exploratorium.edu/chocolate
The history of chocolate and factory tours explaining how it is made.

chocolate.scream.org
The chocolate lover's page with links to 774 chocolate sites around the world.

Mmmmm. Now that we no longer "break out" when eating chocolate we can indulge our passion whenever we like or at least whenever we need a reward for a 10 mile bike ride or fierce aerobic session. You don't still "break out" do you?

Dining Out Restaurant Guide

There are so many restaurants out there that it is comforting to have a few guides to help you pick the good ones. You should eat out every week, right, not just on birthdays, Mother's Day and anniversaries.

www.zagat.com
Zagat is the world's best restaurant review guide. It uses reader's ratings to rank the restaurants and I have seldom known it to be wrong. It's unfortunate that only major cities are covered.

www.food.com
Takeout or delivery from thousands of restaurants near your home.

www.restaurants.com
A list of restaurants in cities across the country and maps to help you find each.

www.fodors.com/ri.cgi
Fodor's expert restaurant reviews for restaurants in the cities they cover. You won't find every one listed but they tend to find the better places.

www.dinesite.com
Restaurants listed by location and broken down by cuisine and type. The ratings seemed to be very generous.

www.restaurantrow.com
Would you believe 100,000 restaurants listed in 24 countries. You could starve to death just deciding which to visit.

www.menusonline.com
A great restaurant guide for 16 major cities with menus, reviews. directions and even dress codes.

ine

- •••⦂ **www.winespectator.com**
  The online version of Wine Spectator magazine. The wine basics are excellent for the unknowledgeable and will really teach you about wine.

- •••⦂ **www.drinkwine.com**
  This site has all sorts of information for the wine lover from food pairings to wine tours to growing your own.

- •••⦂ **www.vine2wine.com**
  A comprehensive wine site that connects you to everything.

- •••⦂ **www.wineculture.com**
  A hip guide to choosing, storing, buying, serving, and saving what's left.

- •••⦂ **www.tablewine.com**
  This site discusses affordable wines, around $10, with different topics each month.

- •••⦂ **www.wineauthority.com**
  Very authoritative and insightful wine reviews.

At 50 some of us have graduated from the screw top caps and straw Chianti bottles that we used to stick candles in at college. Some may even have become wine snobs with different glasses for each variety of grape and a descriptive vocabulary of tastes that sounds like a botany textbook interspersed with a barrel maker's inventory list. The sites shown here are for us 50 year olds in the middle who enjoy a good bottle of wine and haven't yet started annoying our friends with flowery descriptions.

Wine

Pick up a few terms from these wine sites and you can probably match wits with your friends who are wine experts. I like reading wine reviews but I can never find any of the bottles reviewed when I go to a wine shop. I wonder if everyone has this problem. Don't let price influence your buying decisions. Expensive wines rarely come out on top in blind taste tests. Anyone can find a great $100 bottle of wine. The trick is finding a great $10 bottle.

www.thewinenews.com
This wine magazine reviews over a hundred wines each month and I particularly like the double blind nature of their tastings.

clifty.com/wine
A great wine tasting site run by regular folks like you and me and, in fact, here is a place where you can post your own ratings.

www.wineenthusiastmag.com
The Wine Enthusiast magazine, rating and selling everything that has to do with wine.

www.homearts.com/helpers/winenav/wine1.htm
The Wine Navigator has a good wine glossary and information on choosing wine and matching it to food.

www.bandc.com
Reading this informative wine education site of over 200 pages will leave you sober enough to drive home.

www.stratsplace.com/wine.shtml
A superb site with thousands of the usual but also neat stuff like uses for corks, removing wine stains and printing wine tasting sheets.

Cooking Gear

www.cookswares.com
Anything you can think of for preparing food. Their catalog is staggeringly comprehensive and their tips and advice excellent.

www.gourmetpalace.com
Pots and pans and everything else for your kitchen in a well organized site.

www.chefscatalog.com
High end cooking supplies for you gals who are almost pros.

www.kitchenetc.com
Over 23,000 items. How many pots do you need anyway?

www.pattycakes.com
More baking and cake decorating supplies than you knew existed.

www.chocolate-making.com
Grandma's candy and chocolate making supplies. Invite me over to taste the broken pieces.

www.cooking.com
The master site for cooking with lots of cooking gear for sale as well as recipes, products and techniques.

I like to buy cooking gear the same way my husband buys tools. You may never use them but they're good to have "just in case". There are hours of fun here with magnificent new cooking sets and specialized gadgets to make any little doo dad.

Cooking Schools

If cooking is your thing, treat yourself and go to a real school. To be perfectly honest most of these are set up as a short vacation at some very enticing locations. You probably deserve it so don't be embarrassed to go for it.

www.worldtable.com/reports/ecole.html
Week long courses at elegant cooking schools in France.

www.cpv.it/courses/chianti/index.html
Here you can learn Italian cooking while you sip Chianti in Tuscany.

www.cci-oise.fr/infath/index.html
This one is for real. A 14 week course that will make you a French chef. The facilities are at the Baroness James de Rothchilds, Le Manoir.

www.learningvacations.com
Learning Vacations has cooking schools in Greece, Mexico and Italy. If you get tired of the kitchen they have golf schools also.

cookforfun.shawguides.com
There are very long lists of cooking schools for fun and for serious at locations around the world.

www.cookingschools.com
Search here from among 1,000 cooking schools.

Sports

Sports will keep you young and healthy. You know all those articles you're reading about exercising? Well besides walking or working out on a boring gym machine this is what they are talking about. It's time to get into a sport and there are lots of practical ones available. This is probably not the age to get into gymnastics or rock climbing though plenty of 50 year olds do. You'll want to pick something where you won't have to spend several days with Advil and hot baths after each session. The most fun way to get exercise is to participate in some sport and here are a selection to pique your interest.

Golf

Of all the activities suited to 50 year olds, golf is one of the best. While the psychological frustration level can be extreme, the physical stress level is safe, the camaraderie superb and the enjoyment after a winning day sublime. These sites will keep you up-to-date with the sport as well as providing information on courses all over the world.

www.golfweb.com
Golf lessons online along with lots of tournament information, gear ratings, and a pro shop.

www.golfcourse.com
Reviews on over 16,000 courses. "So much golf so little time."

golfcircuit.com/cgi-bin/datasearch/bottom.html
Stats from the circuit, instruction, a golf search engine, plus the inevitable pro shop.

www.msnbc.com/news/golf1_front.asp
NBC Sport's golf coverage with all the latest results.

www.pgaonline.com
The official PGA site with audio coverage of the championships.

golf.traveller.com/golf
Traveler's golf information center with 2,000 courses, scorecard archives, and golf associations.

Golf Equipment

www.golfandtennisworld.com
Golf and Tennis equipment. They promise lowest prices and over 20,000 items in stock. No way you could lose that many balls.

www.mvp.com
High quality golf and other sports equipment along with expert advice on what to buy.

www.clubstest.com
They claim unbiased ratings of all golf clubs plus up to the minute tournament stats and leader-boards.

www.mygolf.com
They sure have a load of golf products and claim the lowest prices on the web.

www.golfcoop.com
This is a non profit coop of golfers who have banded together to get the best prices for their group. You have to register before getting the prices.

Buying the equipment is as much fun as playing to many people and finding the latest club that is going to enhance your game or the ball guaranteed to fly further proba-bly occupies more of these folk's time than lessons. If you're one of them, and I count myself among you, these sites will be a joy.

Golf Magazines

There are many golf magazines and, in addition to news about the sport, they are a wonderful source for tips on improving your game. I, for one, could never get anything out of pictures of swings and hip rotations and weight shifts but perhaps you can understand this stuff.

www.golfdigest.com
Golf Digest's online site with more golf information than you can use.

www.golftoday.co.uk
Europe's premier online golf magazine.

www.golfmagazine.com
Golf Magazine's online site. If you have a day too rainy to play you can easily spend it surfing this site.

www.seniorgolfer.com
I don't know if we are seniors yet but if we are here is a magazine just for you.

www.golfandtravel.com
There are some incredibly beautiful photos on this site and you are going to want to visit them.

www.golfillustrated.com
There seem to be more golf magazines than telephone solicitors at dinner time. The sites don't carry the entire publication but you can probably get all the information you'll ever need by just scanning several of them.

www.womensgolftoday.com
Women's Golf Today magazine where they don't even allow men.

Biking

www.biking.com
Ten thousand bike products for sale plus biking articles and people.

www.dfwnetmall.com/cybersports/bicycle.htm
An introduction to biking for novices including buying a bike, maintenance and other information.

www.bicyclingmagazine.com
Online version of the leading biking magazine.

www.cycling.org
This is quite a site and can link you to any manufacturer as well as provide directions to any bike shop.

www.backroads.com
Backroads offers the largest and among the best bike tours worldwide.

www.gorp.com/gorp/activity/biking/bik_guid.htm
An excellent guide to bike trails and tours throughout the U.S.

www.sevencycles.com
They are expensive, but these guys make the best custom bikes in the world. I own one.

It's your choice. You can be efficient with an aerodynamic position, hard seat, stiff bike and sore body, or comfy with an upright position and plush equipment. I bike a great deal and now that I'm 50 I find myself bending, reluctantly, in the direction of comfort. You probably will also.

Running

This was called jogging when we were younger but now it's running even though we've slowed down to what could be called jogging at best. It wouldn't seem you'd need lots of equipment and information to just run but that's the kind of world we live in now. There are special shoes, special shorts, magazines, coaches and heart monitors just to mention a few.

www.running.com
This site leads you to just about everything you could ever need to know about running.

www.americanrunning.org
The American Running Assoc. hosts a terrific site that lets you easily find information on all aspects of running, equipment and training.

www.runningnetwork.com
An excellent review of running shoes.

www.runningtips.com
Some good basic running tips.

runningshoes.com/hp.php3
Prices on some major brands of running shoes.

Weight and Strength Training

•••:• members.xoom.com/duranman
A good introduction to strength training and bodybuilding.

•••:• www.worldguide.com/Fitness/stex.html
More strength training exercises, with instructions and photos, than you could do in a month of Sundays.

•••:• www.lastingresults.com
This site offers very concise and sound advice and a very practical list of 10 weight exercises.

**•••:• www.thriveonline.com/shape/weights/
weights.intro.html**
Eight essential good basic weight exercises for beginners.

•••:• www.naturalstrength.com
The source for strength training information with no hype and no bull.

After 50, the bones in your body start to thin and the danger of osteoporosis increases. The most efficient way to prevent this and to exercise the hundreds of muscles in your body is by lifting weights. Strength training will likely mean the difference between a frail old age and a vibrant one. Learn something about it here.

Scuba Diving and Snorkeling

Scuba diving and snorkeling are great sports for 50 year olds. They are relatively stress free on your muscle and bone structure and health wise all you have to worry about is being eaten by sharks, having your ear drums blown out and drowning a black horrible death. Fortunately these things don't happen too often and thankfully not, so far, on any of my dives.

•••⦂ **www.scubacentral.com**
A good general site that has a tremendous amount of information including equipment reviews, learning to dive, places to dive, chat, and great photographs.

•••⦂ **www.mtsinai.org/pulmonary/books/scuba/contents.htm**
This is a very comprehensive book that explains all aspects of scuba diving.

•••⦂ **www.scubadiving.com/gear**
Rodale's Scuba Diving Magazine site with excellent reviews of equipment and dive spots along with articles on photography and all aspects of the sport.

•••⦂ **www.padi.com**
Padi, one of the main certification services, maintains this site with information on diving travel and all of their courses.

•••⦂ **www.3routes.com/scuba/index.html**
This site tries to list every dive resort and live aboard in the world. They list over 4,000 and have reviews of many.

Tennis

www.cnnsi.com/tennis

Sport Illustrated and CNN combine to provide tennis news, results, personalities and stories.

www.fogdog.com/pid/GTT/nav/stores/tennis/index.html

Every conceivable kind of tennis equipment. They sell 41 different racquets alone.

www.tennis.com

This online tennis magazine has the usual news, equipment and classified stuff but also an incredibly detailed instruction section on every shot in the game.

www.tennisone.com/lessonshome.html

An absolute library of free tennis instruction. It'll take you all winter to read this material.

www.tennislovers.com/Content/elbow.htm

Tips on preventing and handling "tennis elbow" along with lots more information on gear, rules, clubs and everything else you can think of relating to tennis.

www.tennisweek.com

This magazine gives rankings, news, chat, tips for improving your game and all the rest.

I don't think many people take up tennis at 50. The sudden starting and stopping can be dangerous, but if you are already a player or love to watch the game these sites will provide the information.

erobic Exercise

This is still one of the easiest types of workouts to stick with. It doesn't, after all, rain inside the gyms. Aerobic exercise is what keeps your heart ticking and, of all your activities, this is the single most important. Some of these sites sell programs and music so you can do the workout at home but it is tougher to keep motivated all by yourself.

www.cybercise.com/dyna.html
All kinds of music for aerobic exercising in case you don't already have enough tapes and disks.

www.fitness-factory.com/english/index.html
You can download choreography videos here and they must give the cost somewhere but it was hidden too well for me to find.

www.bodytrends.com/gourley.htm
Basic aerobic exercise principles. This is good information.

www.iwr.com/chimachine
This is another lulu. You buy this "Chi Machine" for only $480 and you plug it in and lie down and 5 minutes is equal to a mile walk. If you accidentally fall asleep you could end up in China.

http://k2.kirtland.cc.mi.us/~balbachl/cardio.htm
A simple and factual explanation about using aerobic exercises to lose weight.

mrmac-jr.scs.unr.edu/jenscott/Fitness.html
It'll take you a minute to read the ten reasons why aerobic exercise is important and they're all true.

Good Things for Women to Know

• • •⋮ **www.howstuffworks.com**
The How Stuff Works site will make you seem like a genius. It tells you how everything works and your kids and friends will think you're absolutely wonderful.

• • •⋮ **www.britannica.com**
The whole Encyclopedia Britannica. What more could you ask for as an information source. I wonder what ever happened to all those people who used to sell them door to door?

• • •⋮ **www.wackyuses.com**
You'll impress everyone when you show them how Coca Cola® can clean a toilet bowl, you can shave with peanut butter, use Jello® to style your hair and Miracle Whip® to remove chewing gum or dead skin.

• • •⋮ **www.virtualflowers.com**
Send virtual flowers, for free, to your mom or friend. They'll love it.

• • •⋮ **www.urbanlegends.com/index.html**
Hundreds of all those crazy stories you've been hearing all your life like alligators living in sewers and cow tipping and Spanish Fly are investigated and discussed, and mostly debunked here.

We're moms and women and we're 50. We have to know all about whatever kids and men and younger people ask especially if it has to do with health or food or how things perform. These sites will give you enough information so you can bluff your way out of almost any question.

Maps

Since your guy probably refuses to ask directions, someone has to have the intelligence to plan and have maps on hand so you can eventually get places. You can buy or download the maps from listed sites here and you'll be delighted to actually arrive on time and without getting lost and with a minimum of arguments should a man be along.

www.mapquest.com
Not only maps of every place but a detailed visitor's guide for everything you'll need from hotels to theaters once you get there.

www.maps.com
If you need to buy folding maps this site has plenty for sale as well as an atlas that pinpoints what's available for any country.

www.maps.expedia.com/OverView.asp
A great site that lays out a map giving you accurate directions between any two points in North America. See if it gets you home by an efficient route.

www.mapblast.com/mblast/index.mb
Free maps and driving directions to all points in the U.S.

geog.gmu.edu/projects/maps/cartogrefs.html
This cartography resource has links to almost 100 internet map sites.

oddens.geog.uu.nl/index.html
This site has links to almost 10,000 map resources. If you can't find it here you probably don't want to go there.

Maps

www.library.yale.edu/MapColl/online.html
A neat site showing pictures of Yale University's historical map collection for the period 1500 to 1900.

hum.amu.edu.pl/~zbzw/glob/glob1.htm
Several hundred great images of the globe with fantastic space views, maps of surface temperatures, glaciers, fires, winds, everything.

www.mapsonus.com
This great site will draw a map of any address you type in or plan you a route between any two points.

www.nationalgeographic.com/resources/ngo/maps
National Geographic's site of maps and flags and world information.

www.nationalatlas.gov
U.S. Geological Survey shows just how much fun you can have with your tax dollars. Play with maps of all the U.S.

terraserver.microsoft.com/default.asp
This neat site lets you view an aerial view of anyplace in the country. Keep zooming in until you can see your own house.

There are lots of places to get maps online and if you want to stay in control of things you should use these sources. You can have hours of fun as well as finding your way to a friend's new house.

Good Information Sources

Besides knowing all about health and food things you can really impress people with knowing how to find zip codes and addresses, weather, traffic and the correct postage to put on a package to Finland. It's all here.

www.usps.gov
The post office site with prices and rates. Find out what that airmail letter to Afghanistan should cost.

www.reversephonedirectory.com
Have a friend's phone number, but need their address? Use the Reverse Phone Directory. Also great if you have Call Identifier and want to know who called you while you were out.

www.usps.gov/ncsc/lookups/lookup_zip+4.html
Need someone's zip code? Just enter the address, and you'll come up with their zip code + 4 as well as their county.

www.smartraveler.com
Traffic updated frequently for major cities in the US, with links to city-related travel services.

www.govworks.com
This site offers a free service finding information or answering questions about any of your governmental needs.

Film and Video Reviews

- **www.imdb.com**
  A data base of every film released since the beginning of the century. This may be the best movie and video site on the web. They even tell you how to sell your old videos.

- **www.filmgeek.com**
  Very complete reviews of new film and video releases.

- **www.film.com**
  In depth reviews of current films, and there are more than you can imagine, plus any video you can think of.

- **mrshowbiz.go.com**
  Another wonderful entertainment site with TV ratings as well as films and videos.

- **www.movie-reviews.com**
  Excellent and easy to use film and video reviews with star ratings.

Why go to lousy films and rent boring videos just to please others. Get the real ratings and reviews at these sites and make your own decisions. By God if you want to see a movie that makes you cry you should be able to.

Film and Video Reviews

It's fun, after 50 years of seeing films, to look at lists of the best ones and reminisce about drive ins and high school romances and realize just how many you've seen or missed.

•••• **www.filmsite.org**
The Greatest Films specializes in classics. Wonderful descriptions of their top 100.

•••• **www.reel.com**
Good reviews of current films as well as videos and DVD's.

•••• **entertainment.msn.com/movies/movies.asp**
Just type in your zip code and it will give you theaters and showtimes.

•••• **www.video-reviewmaster.com**
Over 225,000 actual movie reviews (I didn't check them all) plus over 45,000 titles available.

•••• **www.rarecelebs.net**
Here is the place to track down rare celebrities about whom you'd like more information.

Politics

- **www.e-thepeople.com**
  No need to go to rallies and risk freezing or even being beaten by the authorities like in the 60's. With this site you can pick an issue right on line and enter your petition.

- **www.politicaljunkie.com**
  Everything political is on this site. Perspectives, facts and figures, people and organizations, newspapers, government, everything.

- **www.thenewrepublic.com**
  Washington insider news and thoughtful articles on politics and foreign affairs.

- **politics.slate.msn.com/politics**
  Top stories and politics from around the country.

- **www.politics1.com**
  Links to all the political parties, issues and debates, all political news sources, state races and campaign consultants.

- **www.democracynet.org**
  A public interest site for election information. The site is nonpartisan and funded by foundations.

The internet makes it not only easier to keep up with politics but you can also take an active role without leaving your computer. This will probably grow in the future until some hackers learn how to rig a poll.

Weather

Remember how old people were always worrying about the weather? When people move to Florida they still delight in telling you just how cold it was last night in New England or wherever else you live. The advent of "wind chill" thrills anyone who lives in a warm climate and has relatives in the cold and a telephone to reach them with.

www.accuweather.com/weatherf/index_corp
It's fun to enlarge and animate the map.

www.weather24.com
Weather24 will send the forecast to your email address so you'll always have the latest info.

www.intellicast.com
Weather and forecasts anyplace in the world.

iwin.nws.noaa.gov/iwin/graphicsversion/ rbigmain.html
The most complete, statistic laden, boring and hard to understand site, courtesy of your National Weather Service.

www.weather.com
Just fill in the zip code and up comes the weather. World weather as well and moving satellite pictures.

weather.yahoo.com/index.html
Current weather and 4 day forecasts. Weather maps, worldwide weather, ski reports etc.

www.washingtonpost.com/wp-srv/weather/histor-ical/historical.htm
Historical weather for over 2,000 cities. Record highs, lows, rain, clouds, snow and everything else you can think of.

www.ncdc.noaa.gov/extremes.html
U.S. weather extremes and global historical records like 523 inches of rain in Columbia and 136 degrees in Libya.

Music for 50 Year Olds

•••• **www.oldiesmusic.com**
On this site you can search oldies music of the 50's, 60's, and 70's. This is the good stuff that you can dance to, sing to and fall in love with.

•••• **www.on-air.com**
An internet-only radio station where you can hear all your old favorites.

•••• **www.srv.net/~roxtar/oldies.html**
Reviews of songs and artists from your formative years. You'll enjoy seeing the old names.

•••• **www.wanderers.com/wanderer**
Over 900 full length stereo oldies from the 50's, 60's and early 70's plus TV themes and commercials from the period.

•••• **www.on-air.com**
An internet radio station with channels of music from our period.

•••• **tdm.net/oldies**
The official Oldies Music Ring where you'll find a bunch of sites about the music you remember.

•••• **www.geocities.com/SunsetStrip/Alley/4795/links.htm**
Over 100 links to find The Beatles, ABBA, Simon and Garfunkle, The Rolling Stones and everyone else.

You've probably learned by now that "your music" isn't "their" music. Young people probably laugh at your taste in music but they are likely already too deaf to realize how great it is. Listed here are some places you can find just what you like.

Music for 50 Year Olds

Some people say that if you expect to go to heaven you'd better get used to classical music. Here are your information sources for classical and Christian music.

www.allmusic.com
An incredibly comprehensive source of music information. Hundreds of thousands of reviews and audio samples and you can search for anything in 6 languages.

www.cmo.com/cmo/index.html
All sorts of information on Christian music: concerts, artists, sound files.

www.classical.net
A wonderful guide to classical music with reviews, basic repertoire guide, guide to composers and much more.

www.stagebill.com
An excellent guide to the performing arts across the country: opera, jazz, dance, theater, classical. Just type in your city and what you'd like to hear.

www.classicaliscool.com
Find quality music with radio stations and concerts throughout the country.

rt

- **www.artchive.com**

  An archive of over 2,000 works of art from over 200 artists with commentaries and galleries. The scans are excellent and you don't have to worry about crowds at your local museum.

- **www.wwar.com**

  A worldwide art resource that allows you to search galleries, artists, museums etc. There are for example 945 museums in the U.S. alone which should keep you busy for a few weekends.

- **www.artresources.com**

  Articles, reviews and guides to shows, museums and galleries plus over 2,000 images in their catalog.

- **www.art.com**

  Extensive art and poster collection searchable by artist, subject or color.

- **www.artcyclopedia.com**

  Browse by name or other searches to find any artist. Their top 30 artists, based on web popularity, is fascinating.

- **www.artlex.com**

  A visual arts dictionary of art-related terms that will allow you to hold your own at a cocktail party made up entirely of art historians.

The internet is a perfect place to learn about and get information on all forms of art and I hope you have a fast method of downloading the pictures. Slow connections make the internet much less fun.

Art

The richest, most powerful kings and rulers of the past could not have a fraction of the art available to you with only a few clicks on your computer. You should absolutely glory at the overwhelming amount of beauty and information that is available for your poor brain to absorb.

witcombe.sbc.edu/ARTHLinks.html
A truly overwhelming site that categorizes and breaks down art by period, style and country and has incredible detail on each.

www.artmuseum.net
Almost as much fun as a trip to a great museum. This Intel sponsored site offers excellent quality tours of major exhibits.

www.art.net
Wandering through this site is like visiting the world's largest art colony as artists share their work with you. Sculptors, painters, digital artists and every other kind are all represented.

www.amn.org
The official exhibition calendar of the world's leading art museums.

www.nga.gov
The National Gallery of Art has weekly tours which are a lovely way to spend a little time.

www.metmuseum.org
You can view exhibits from the Metropolitan Museum of Art and I hope you have a 17 inch screen because these are magnificent to see.

Find Your Old Friends

•••• **www.infospace.com**
Just type in the last and first name and, by God, they usually come up. You can also search public records to find them especially if they still owe you money.

•••• **www.theultimates.com**
This site searches by several engines and if you use it a lot will give more features and better service for 12 bucks a year.

•••• **www.knowx.com/free/peoplefinder.htm**
This ultimate people finder uses real estate and change of address records as well as phone books to find the long lost ones.

•••• **www.worldemail.com**
A world email directory with 18 million listings in 6 different languages.

•••• **www.reunion.com**
An online missing persons bulletin board and registry. Maybe someone out there is looking for you.

•••• **www.search-shark.com**
A serious people searcher that uses military records, Social Security numbers, death notices and public records as well as the usual.

There are lots of people-finding facilities on the internet and it's a hoot to look up old friends. Find that snitch from the sixth grade or your old high school flame. Let them know how successful you've become.

Genealogy

Find out if your man is right and you really are a Princess. Perhaps there are nobles among your ancestors and maybe even a castle or crown waiting for you in Slobania. ●●●

www.cyndislist.com
> The most spectacular genealogy site on the web. Your one stop spot for more than 63,000 links most of which are categorized and cross-referenced in over 120 categories, such as country or religion. Constantly updated.

www.familysearch.org/sg/DisTree.html
> This Mormon site is the foremost source of genealogical records. An excellent way to begin your search with information on methods, addresses of sources, and untold helpful hints.

www.ancestry.com/search/main.htm
> Constantly updated database of over 500 million names. The information is only available to those who join at a fee, but, if you're intent on tracing your family, this is the place to go.

www.oz.net/~markhow/ukbegin.htm
> Beginning genealogic research for England and Wales. Links to civil registrations, census returns, parish registers, books and other internet links.

www.jewishgen.org
> Primary internet source connecting researchers of Jewish genealogy worldwide. Contains a database of over 175,000 surnames and towns, ShtetLinks for over 200 communities, and a variety of databases.

www.polishroots.com/genpoland/index.htm
> If your family came from Poland, this is an excellent place to begin research into your family's history.

www.geocities.com/SiliconValley/Haven/1538/germ_rus.html
> List of German-Russian Genealogy Links.

www.irish-insight.com/a2z-genealogy
> Over three hundred Links to genealogy of Ireland and Northern Ireland.

S hopping

www.catalogsite.com
A cataloging of catalogs. Over 200 catalogs shown by the top 10 or by interest.

www.theoutdoorwoman.com
Women's sporting apparel and accessories. Even if you don't hunt or fish you can look cool and impress your friends.

www.silhouettes.com
A large selection for full figured women.

www.styleclick.com
Search through hundreds of brands in this online catalog each showing their line. It would seem this site could clothe the world.

www.coach.com/index.asp
The Coach leathers are not cheap, my God they had a $58 key chain, but they are well made and beautiful.

www.tallclassics.com
If you are over 5' 10" this is the place for you.

www.longelegantlegs.com
Another site for tall gals in case the one above doesn't have your color.

As long as those credit card offers keep coming through the mail it means you still have credit available so you might as well keep going until they tell you to stop. You can do it all right from your home. For items where fit or feel are not critical it's an easy way to spend too much.

Clothes and Fashion

You may not be able to try on things but for garments where you need a large selection of sizes and colors the internet is pretty handy. Don't worry too much about the security of your credit card. It's probably safer than handing it to some teenage drugy in a record store.

fashion.about.com/style/fashion/msub13.htm
There is so much on this site I always find it a little overwhelming but the advice and tips and fashion trends are sound.

www.wwd.com
Women's Wear Daily. The horse's mouth.

www.godess.com
Detailed global fashion news. You can also click around and get world news from anywhere.

www.worldmedia.fr/fashion
Haute couture designers and their collections.

www.fashion.net
Fashion news, chat, runway videos and shopping.

www.apparel.net/index.cgi
What's new, what's cool, designers, catalogs, manufacturers and lots of clothing.

www.7thonsixth.com
One of those pain in the behind sites that you can't get rid of. I think it has information on all the fashion shows. Don't bother unless you're ready to unplug your computer.

Household Furniture

- **www.crateandbarrel.com**
  Furniture and accessories for your home from Crate and Barrel.

- **www.homefurnish.com/buy_menu.htm**
  A guide to understanding the quality of wood and upholstered furniture as well as what different pieces are best for.

- **www.cherryhillfurn.com/c3.html**
  Some more good advice on understanding furniture and what to look for in determining quality.

- **www.furnishingsfinder.com**
  This is a useful site. Pick the room, furniture and price you're looking for and up pops a list of manufacturer's sites to visit.

- **www.geocities.com/Heartland/7400/furniture.html**
  How to buy furniture at discount prices from all the main manufacturers in North Carolina.

- **www.ianr.unl.edu/pubs/homefurnish/g1247.htm**
  Excellent discussion of what to look for and how wood furniture is made.

- **www.furniture.com**
  You can view much more furniture on a site like this than any store can carry. It's an excellent way to plan.

> You won't sit in the chair or slide out the drawers but you can't beat the selection and prices. After you know exactly what you want it's worth checking out the prices.

Shopping Malls

These malls are trying to offer everything you need in one location. The concept is viable but I think most of them need a little more time pulling it all together. Right now you'll probably find a better selection going to specialists in a particular category.

galaxymall.com
Their extensive links take you to every imaginable kind of goods and service.

www.all-internet.com
Over 150,000 shopping pages. I didn't check them all out.

www.icw.com/ams.html
As much fun as going to outlet stores. Just endless things you'd never think you'd need.

www.buyitonline.com/home.asp
There certainly is a lot for sale on the web.

www.fashionmall.com
Designer brands from top designers as well as sneak previews.

www.olworld.com/mall/mall_us/index.html
This world mall offers 19 categories from stores in Europe, Australia, UK and US and has some new and different stuff.

www.buyerszone.com
If you need anything for your business this is without a doubt the best site on the internet for educating you and helping you pick brands.

Car Buying Information

• **www.autosite.com**
A great site with dealer invoice prices, used car values, photos, specs and everything else to help you buy a car.

• **www.aautomall.com**
Automall searches over 600 dealers and lets you email them for quotes on the car you want. It also has information on warranties, insurance and everything else involved with buying a car.

• **www.caranddriver.com**
Car and Driver magazine's online site with excellent car reviews and articles. Check out their 10 best cars of the year.

• **www.autobytel.com**
Invoice prices, safety records and car reviews make it easy for you to buy a car.

• **www.dealernet.com**
There are almost 7,000 dealers represented here. Check out free quotes from one near your home.

• **www.nhtsa.dot.gov**
Your government provides lots of information on the safety of vehicles and other life saving concerns. It is worth checking out before selecting a car.

• **www.kbb.com**
The famous Kelly Blue Book which gives you the used car values that the dealers laugh at and you can never get when you try to sell it yourself.

• **www.carorder.com**
You can pick the options you want and actually buy the car at this site.

If the sales people treated you like an idiot the last time you bought a car, check out a few of these sites and go for your test drive armed with the dealer cost and knowledge of all the options you don't want. They'll probably treat you the same but if you get really annoyed you can always order from the internet.

How your Car Works

You probably don't want to repair the old buggy yourself but you can get enough free advice to figure out what's wrong and at least talk intelligently with the Service Manager for all the good that usually does a woman.

••••• **www.womanmotorist.com**
The Woman Motorist site will teach you all about car maintenance and technology.

••••• **www.cskauto.com**
Maintenance tips and parts in case you're really serious about doing this yourself.

••••• **www.autosite.com/garage/garmenu.asp**
With this repair encyclopedia and troubleshooting guide you could even fix it yourself.

••••• **www.allexperts.com/browse.asp?Meta=12**
An incredibly valuable site where you can submit questions on car repair and get an email response from experts.

••••• **www.autorepairconsultant.net**
A free general question consulting service that will answer your questions by email. They charge $25 for specific printed material and training.

Bathroom Remodeling

•••• **www.kitchen-bath.com/bbasics.htm**
   Bathroom design basics in case you are seriously interested in a remodeling job.

•••• **www.us.amstd.com/scripts**
   If you want to view some luxury bathrooms the American Standard site is a nice place to start your dreaming.

•••• **www.hometime.com/projects/ktchbath.htm**
   All the how-to information if you are planning to remodel your bathroom. Don't forget the saunas, spas and steam rooms.

•••• **www.nkba.org**
   The National Kitchen and Bath Assoc. gives you worthwhile tips on remodeling as well as links to manufacturers.

•••• **www.bathweb.com**
   A complete directory to the bathroom industry. You can find everything here including group bathtubs.

If you are like me, you spend many happy hours in your bathroom either contemplating weighty matters, reading, wallowing in a tub or pampering yourself. There is no sense spending all this time in uncomfortable surroundings and these sites will show you just what kind of luxury is available. It's a good place to spend money since all real estate brokers say it increases the value of your home.

Kitchen Remodeling

Even if you don't build your dream kitchen immediately it's fun to go to these sites and do some dreaming. The sites that help you design a kitchen based on its functions will even help you to reorganize your present space to be more efficient.

- **www.improvenet.com/Dream/DesignGallery/DG1.html?sp=1**
  An excellent source for planning your new kitchen.

- **www.ikitchendesign.com**
  A great guide to kitchen remodeling. It will help organize and direct all your thoughts.

- **www.homeideas.com**
  Just check off the catalogs you want and they will send them to you by mail. Very comprehensive.

- **www.kitchen-bath.com/hotstuff.htm**
  This site helps you find sources for cabinets, appliances or anything else your kitchen needs.

- **www.tapdirect.com/kitchentips.htm**
  Kitchen remodeling secrets and tips for $39.95 plus free links to many suppliers most of whom have nothing to do with kitchens.

- **www.hometime.com/projects/howto/kitchen/pc2kit01.htm**
  An excellent discussion of how to lay out a kitchen considering the 3 basic functions of storage, preparation and cleanup.

- **www.remodelonline.com/directories/construction/kitchen**
  Directories to everything you could possibly need for remodeling a kitchen.

Landscaping

- **www.landscapeweb.com**
  Lots of sources for landscaping of such things as fences and gates, irrigation, ponds, outdoor sculpture and more.

- **aggie-horticulture.tamu.edu/extension/ homelandscape/home.html**
  A great place to get advice on developing your landscaping plan and creating the visual relationship between your house and site.

- **www.markw.com/10point.htm**
  An excellent 10 point landscaping guide for home buyers that will also educate you on intelligent landscaping.

- **www.lotf.com**
  Pictures of some beautiful landscaping designs and information on construction, plants, bugs etc.

- **www.tcp.ca/Jan95/Gardening.html**
  If you are interested in landscaping software to help with your design, this site reviews and recommends different brands that cost around $50.

- **www.clearwaterlandscapes.com**
  Landscaping design online and free landscaping tips.

I always think of landscaping as gardening on a grander and more functional scale. You can plan the shrubs and trees around your home to provide flowering beauty or cool shade or screening. If you're smart you'll hire some strong kid to do the real digging.

105

Pastimes, Interests, and Hobbies

Hobbies may sound a little juvenile for a 50 year old but we all have these little collections and interests and I guess they qualify as hobbies for lack of a better word. And when dignified with the title "hobby" there is much less chance your mate will want to put the collection in the garage to make more space for his junk.

Photography

•••• www.photography.com
A pleasant site with a good "Ask the Pro" section, photo news, search provisions and a daily contest.

•••• www.onlinephotography.com
This site has some gorgeous photos and a well done, if limited, product review section.

•••• www.kodak.com/US/en/nav/takingPics.shtml
Kodak's classic Guide To Better Pictures. This advice is so sound and so basic it makes you wonder why 95% of the photo-taking public ignores it. Worth reading and rereading.

•••• www.bath.ac.uk/~masres/photo/manual.html
A good basic introduction to photography. Email this to your friends who are not good photographers and looking at their pictures will be much less painful.

•••• home.netcom.com/~nikonman/phototips1.html
Very sound tips from a pro. This site is eminently readable and full of good ideas.

Everybody is a photographer and if everybody would just look at a few of these sites and learn how to really use their cameras we'd all be a lot less bored looking at everybody's boring pictures.

Gardening

This subject is covered in detail on the internet and there are innumerable sites. I've just listed a few to help you get started but if you need more just type in "Gardening" and you'll be still reading while your garden withers away from lack of attention

www.garden.org
The National Gardening Association has articles, tips and answers to your questions.

www.garden.com
A good place to buy 20,000 different products for your garden. Beautiful photos.

www.gardenguides.com
Wonderful garden guides to everything you may want to plant plus lists of mostly free catalogs.

www.gardenweb.com
Lots of gardening resources are listed here with links to specialties such as Kitchen Gardens and Wildflowers. There are sections on seed exchanges and a botany glossary.

www.coronaclipper.com/ornam_trees.htm
Pruning ornamental trees hedges and shrubs.

treeselect.com/treesearch.htm
Here is a great data base of trees categorized by color, shape size, growth rate and everything else you can think of.

Flowers and Gardens

garden-gate.prairienet.org
Links to virtually every type of gardening web site imaginable. A special feature is full-color pictures from world famous gardens.

www.sierra.com/sierrahome/gardening
Very inclusive site with plant encyclopedia, gardening software, timely hints and suggestions.

www.organicgardening.com
Rodale's on-line Organic Gardening Magazine.

www.gardenguides.com
Guide Sheets on every imaginable flower, herb, and vegetable with full color pictures and detailed information on planting and care.

www.io.com/neighbor
The Gardening Launch Pad contains links to all types of flowers and vegetables, magazines, preferred retailers, forums, newsletters, tips by the month.

www.gardennet.com
"The premiere gateway to gardening on the net." With a plant and plant group information section, garden links, garden shop links, garden guidebook of public gardens by State, publications links, discussion area, books.

www.gardenbazaar.com
Listing of garden-related businesses by category. It's a bit random within each category which makes searching somewhat tedious.

While these sites are informative it's not the same as getting your hands dirty in the soil. Don't spend a single sunny day fiddling with your computer when you could be digging.

Dance

We were all ballerinas once (I tap danced) and this is a wonderful way to keep up to date with what's happening or even get inspired to try again.

www.danceonline.com
Contemporary dance news, information, talk reviews and photos.

www.dancer.com/dance-links
All the dance links you could ever need. Ballet, modern, schools, newsgroups, performances, dancers, tap, flamenco, everything.

www.dancemagazine.com
Dance Magazine will keep you up to date on everything that's happening, who's doing what with an extensive calendar.

www.artswire.org/Artswire/www/dance/browse.html
Another master list of seemingly every dance link in the universe. If you can't find it here you don't want to know about it.

www.webcom.com/shownet/kirov/ballink.html
This is the site where I found all the other master links and it links to about 50 sites and you'll be too stiff to dance by the time you check them all.

Bellydancing

•••••• **www.bdancer.com**

Great source for links to everything you might want to know about bellydancing including contacts around the world, the history of belly dancing, commercial links, and regional, troupe, and individual home pages.

•••••• **www.costlesscostumes.com**

Your one-stop shop for a wonderful assortment of bellydancing accouterments. Deck yourself out and you can probably make a fortune dancing at Mideastern restaurants.

•••••• **www.bohemianmarket.com**

The market place of the world! Your connection for Middle Eastern dance supplies, Spanish dance accents, Polynesian trinkets, Renaissance needs, music, and art.

•••••• **www.saroyanzils.com/offset/zills.htm**

Here's the site to find cymbals of every sort and for every level bellydancer.

•••••• **www.visionarydance.com**

Bellydance workshops, instructional videos, retreats, events, festivals and performances.

•••••• **www.sonic.net/~akantor/kajira**

This site contains information about bellydancing, especially of the tribal persuasion. It also has interviews and class schedules and information about the Romany (Gypsy) culture as well.

> Bellydancing at our age? Well, it's great exercise and you'll feel sexy as all getup not to mention driving your man wild. And the outfits will make you the hit of any costume parties.

Birding

Birding is a lifelong quest which fits well into a 50 year old's scheme of things. It's hard to hurt yourself and you get lots of fresh air. Resist trying to set sighting records.

www.gorp.com/gorp/activity/birding.htm
A super birding site with species, regional guide, refuges, links and such.

www.npwrc.usgs.gov/resource/othrdata/chekbird/chekbird.htm
Bird checklists of the United States. Current information on bird distribution throughout the country.

www-stat.wharton.upenn.edu/~siler/birding.html
Birding on the net with a hot list for posting sightings, numerous links and the Sibley-Monroe classification.

www.birdfeeding.org
The National Bird-Feeding Society with bird feeding information unlike anything you've ever seen.

sunsite.sut.ac.jp/multimed/sounds/birds
An archive of bird songs.

www.nmnh.si.edu/BIRDNET
Links to more bird societies and resources than you'll be able to check out.

Knitting

www.redlipstick.net/knit
A lovely non-commercial site with free knitting stitches for hand and machine knitters. Updated monthly.

www.patternworks.com/tools
If you want to have fun looking through knitter's gadgets, tools and supplies this is the site to visit.

knitting.miningco.com/hobbies/knitting
Lots of free patterns broken down by garment type plus links to absolutely every aspect of knitting.

www.learntoknit.com
This is a site for beginning knitters and crocheters giving you the basics and where to find supplies.

www.woolworks.org
Another non-commercial, wonderful site full of information for knitters. There are patterns, resources, stores and links to everything.

members.aol.com/knitnotes/home
Lots of photos, information and links along with a machine knitting web ring.

It's relaxing and productive as you turn out warmth for your children and grandchildren that will grow into treasures. What other hobby can you do under the covers or at movies?

Quilting

Quilts not only keep you warm, the well-made ones become incredibly valuable. Learn to do the well-made ones. If nothing more quilting will clean all the fabric scraps out of your closets.

www.tvq.com
Quilting news, reviews, patterns, product evaluation, and lots of links to quilting information.

ttsw.com/MainQuiltingPage.html
The world's oldest and largest quilting site. Everything from a beginner's guide to a quilting search engine to help you find all the information that is available.

www.quiltart.com
Quite a gallery of magnificent quilts in superb color.

www.piecing.com
America's largest quilt supply store with a free 128 page catalog of everything you'll need.

ares.redsword.com/dduperault/qsource.htm
An excellent source for quilting information, patterns, tips and help. Even a section to help recover stolen quilts.

www.quiltmag.com
Excerpts and articles from 4 quilting magazines that will keep you occupied with ideas and stories.

Antiques

www.curioscape.com
You can browse in over 500 categories of antiques and collectibles. Surely you'll find something of interest.

www.tias.com
You can browse for antiques by category. They claim to have 250,000 items and there is good information on how prices are established.

www.antiqnet.com
A good site to search for stuff in a long list of categories along with dealers and antique centers.

pages.ebay.com/antiques-index.html
You probably know about eBay and this is a brilliantly done antiquing place.

www.seniorssearch.com/santiques.htm
An antique and collectible site specifically for people over 50. Hey, we're already there and they have all the stuff we want.

Antiques are more than elegant collections that you hope will increase in value. They give you good excuses to travel and search and shop. If you specialize, like you're supposed to, every now and then you'll uncover a real treasure.

C ollectibles

This category overlaps of course with antiques, the terms being used casually for things others throw out that we want to keep at least until our kids throw them away. It's best to get involved in a fad early if your interest is in turning a profit. Buying Beanie Babies at the peak is only going to make someone else rich.

communities.msn.com/collectibles
News on what is becoming hot and what you should look for in the back of your garage.

www.mastercollector.com
A large doll and toy collector site.

www.collectiblesnet.com
All the toys, dolls, comics, glass and other junk that you threw out years ago is for sale here. Who kept all this stuff?

www.booksoncollectibles.com
Books on collectibles. You'd better buy some of these before your next trip to the dump or you'll find your heirs buying your own stuff back.

www.classic-cards-gifts.com
All the popular collectibles are here. The Bradford plates, Ty Beanies, Precious Moments etc.

acguide.kaleden.com
An extensive site of antiques and collectibles, shops, dealers, organizations, events and every-thing anyone ever thought of collecting.

Online Book Clubs

bookchatter.com
Books, chosen by members, rated and reviewed by message board, are discussed monthly. Easy to navigate reading and discussion schedule, discussion page, previous reading selections.

books.rpmdp.com
A current reading schedule of books with dates during which discussion takes place via a listserve. You may express your opinion and rate the books. Complete listing of books read and rated for the past 5 years.

www.mindmills.net/booklovers
Discussion list information, author of the month, and a listserve to join their discussion group.

www.aande.com/bookclub
A&E Cable Station book club to discuss both classic and contemporary literature. You have to register, but it is free.

women.com/clubs/book.html
This book club lets you join other bookworms for message board conversations on all sorts of book-related topics and more.

If you like a little interaction and discussion with the books you read, the internet lets you do it on your own schedule and with people whose opinions and ideas you enjoy and it's never your turn to bring the coffee cake.

Literature

These literature sites are as good as going back to school and they can really guide you to some great works. Delve into all the classics that will improve your mind.

authorweb.dingir.org
This site features 500 authors and you can link directly to them and get reviews and ratings of some of their work.

www.promo.net/pg/list.html
Thousands of books can be downloaded for free from this site once you learn how to use the download connections. You probably won't have to buy another book for the rest of your life.

vos.ucsb.edu
An incredible resource for all the humanities. Links to every genre of literature as well as all the humanities. It is hard to imagine one individual developing this site.

andromeda.rutgers.edu/~jlynch/syllabi.html
Syllabi and literature course materials that are available on the web. If you are interested in expanding your knowledge in a particular area this is a great place to start.

englishlit.about.com/arts/englishlit
This is an English literature site but you can explore the classic literature of virtually every other language by clicking on the left hand bar.

www.randomhouse.com/books/bannedbooks
A very long list of books that were banned at one time or the other. A fascinating site and now you can read them all.

Romance and Romance Novels

•••:• **www.writepage.com/romance.htm**
   A list of all the authors, a brief biography and description of their latest works.

•••:• **come.to/romancenovels**
   Lots of links, discussions, reviews, sites of many authors and even a place to trade novels.

•••:• **www.bookbugontheweb.com**
   Up coming releases, top 100 romances, authors' email addresses, reviews and web ring.

•••:• **www.theromancereader.com**
   The very latest news and reviews of romance novels.

•••:• **www.1001waystoberomantic.com/one.html**
   A thousand ways to be romantic plus other neat stuff like the 17 best love songs of all times. The 7 and 8 year old kids' comments on love and marriage (under miscellaneous) are priceless.

•••:• **www.silcom.com/~manatee/underthecovers.html**
   A non commercial site of book reviews by everyday readers.

If we are going to have a page on book clubs and fine literature we have to include some of the fun stuff as well. Here you'll find all your favorite writers and ratings and discussions.

Decorating

When it's time to give the ratty old couch to the Salvation Army and change the color of your curtains check out these sites and become a decorating expert. Everyone's taste is different and all you really need to become an expert is the guts to make decisions.

hg.women.com/homeandgarden/decor/index.htm?msns

Decorating 101. An expert's guide to adorning your abode plus endless decorating information.

interiordec.about.com/homegarden/interiordec

About.com has such complex looking sites that I have stayed away from them but this one certainly has a wonderful list of decorating subjects.

www5.electriciti.com/todesign/report12.htm

This site sells decorating books and they have a free report on defining your style which is an excellent place to start your planning.

www.designaroom.com

What a fun site. You can create a room and fill it with furniture and move everything around to try it all out. Fabulous.

www.isdesignet.com

The online version of Interiors and Sources Magazine. It's for professionals and you'll be one if you read all the articles.

www.dir-dd.com/mainpage.html
Thousands of showpiece images from interior decorators, home furnishing resources, and antique dealers.

www.thehome.com
You will get a wonderful education on this site about furniture, floors and other subjects.

www.furniturefind.com
This is quite an extensive furniture site with excellent pictures of major lines for every room in your house plus electronics and claims of large discounts.

www.decoratingstudio.com
A vast site with lots of advice but also staggeringly complete links to suppliers for everything imaginable in your home.

www.artifice.com/free/dw_lite.html
You can download a free 3-D imaging tool which lets you design a room and look at it from every angle.

www.imsisoft.com/floorplan/products/FPv5.html
This 3-D photo realistic planner costs $49 but it sure beats moving the furniture around as you try to find the best layout.

If you're interested in going into business for yourself think of how much fun you'll have being an interior decorator and shopping with other people's money. Anyone can do it. Just study a few of these sites, swing your arms around a lot and be bold when you tell clients what they should do.

Beauty and Makeup

A seventeen year old complexion rarely hangs around for 50 years with the ravages of sun and wind being what they are. These beauty and makeup tips will give you hope should you be the kind that bothers about these things.

www.women.com/beautifulyou
Real women talk about topics you can really relate to along with beauty and styling tips.

www.beautylink.com
This beauty site gives tips from experts for all your body parts as well as the latest industry gossip and news.

www.adiscountbeauty.com
All the beauty products that you hope will fulfill their claims. At least most of this goo is 40% off.

www.beautyproducts4you.com
They claim to offer tax free beauty products because they are on an Indian reservation. Watch out for the bear grease.

www.just4hair.com
All the salon hair products at discount prices. Is there still room in your shower?

www.fragrancenet.com/html
Can you even imagine 1,200 brands of perfume. They promise up to 70% off.

sflintl.com
Don't miss this one. Guaranteed larger breasts in 90 days with "Wonder Cream". You see, this stuff stimulates your natural hormones and promotes gains of 1 to 3 cup sizes plus it won't stain or smell or make you fat. Only $229.95 (a $40 savings).

www.style-beauty-barber.com/prod01.htm
Thirty thousand (30,000) beauty products. If these can't do something for those bad hair days nothing can.

Family

Up there with your health your family is the most important part of your life so you might as well read a little about these relationships with the help of the internet. Your kids are likely teenagers who will disappear from the human race until it's time to go to college at which time they'll reappear asking for even more money. There is no hope understanding men so I haven't even bothered to list sites dealing with that subject. After you get past kids and grandmothering you might as well skip to your best friend, the dog.

Motherhood

While at 50 you can probably write the book on "motherhood" your kids most likely keep introducing new challenges and it is comforting to chat with other mothers who are dealing with the same lunatic kind of problems.

www.thecybermom.com
A bit commercial looking but a delightful way to connect with other moms and all the things you are interested in.

www.cybermom.com
A nice place for moms to meet and talk about kids, recipes, health, fitness and fun.

www.salon.com/mwt
A site for mothers who think and I think you'll like this place with its articles about family and things in general.

www.epinions.com/book-Family___Relationships-Motherhood
Good reviews on a load of books on motherhood.

www.mom.com
Everything about being a mom: research, opinions and interaction.

childcare-ppin.com
An abundance of articles on a broad range of topics about childcare.

Love and Relationships

•••⦂ **www.topchoice.com/~psyche/love**
Links to various sources of information on love and relationships. Types of love, types of communication, sexuality and compatibility.

•••⦂ **marriage.about.com/people/marriage**
All sorts of tips and thoughts on marriage that are worthwhile discussing with your loved one.

•••⦂ **www.coopcomm.org/fswcover.htm**
A quite good online book on developing skills for better communications with family and friends.

•••⦂ **loveisgreat.com**
The home page is ridiculously hokey but click on "What is True Love" and some fine thoughts come up.

•••⦂ **www.buscaglia.com**
Thoughts on love and loving and life from Dr. Leo Buscaglia.

•••⦂ **www.lovemore.com**
This magazine promotes "Polyamory" which I guess is loving several people at once and seems to lead to some very original family relationships.

If you've made it this far you certainly love each other but like Tevya says in "Fiddler On The Roof" it's still nice to know every now and then.

Interacting With Your Kids - Theme Parks

They may no longer want to confide in you and are mortified over what you say when you drive with their friends and are embarrassed by what you wear and think all your ideas are "dated" but if you invite them to a theme park they will be your best friend. Here are a few.

- **www.screamscape.com**
  A personal guide and best touring tips to parks and attractions. Great reviews of rides.

- **members.aol.com/parklinks/links.htm**
  Absolutely total coverage of the entire theme park, carnival, state/county fairs, fun centers and ride world. They even have accident reports so you can work up your excuses for rides you'd rather skip.

- **www.geocities.com/~robbalvey**
  A couple's guide and ratings of theme parks and roller coasters. And, if you can stand it, 300 photos of their roller coaster honeymoon.

- **users.sgi.net/~rollocst/amuse.html**
  Links to every amusement, theme park, water park and every other kind of fun center you can imagine.

- **themeparks.about.com/travel/themeparks**
  You can find every theme park, roller coaster, zoo and whatever in the world with this site.

Slang and Language

•••• www.slanguage.com
American Slanguage guide that lets you pick a city and talk like the locals or look up the latest teen talk. Dat is crunk.

•••• www.peevish.co.uk/slang
This site lets you plug in a word and find out its meaning. It's from the United Kingdom, where so much slang originated, so they should know.

•••• www.miskatonic.org/slang.html
This claims to be a glossary of hardboiled slang but you'll actually recognize some of the terms. It's a long list and you'll enjoy becoming hip as you face this new language.

•••• www.csupomona.edu/~jasanders/slang
College slang. You'll love the top 20 list because it has every word your kids use and you don't.

•••• www.rapdict.org
This is a serious list of rap slang but I suspect it is out of date by the time it arrives on the internet.

•••• dir.yahoo.com/Reference/Dictionaries/Slang
This site lists a load of slang dictionaries and if you get into them too deeply your own family will no longer understand you.

Are you having trouble understanding your kids? Do they use terms like peeps and warsh and yo sup that you have no idea of the meanings? The sites listed here will make you hip again so you can sound like an idiot teenager whenever you want. Also, don't forget to put your hat on backwards.

Colleges For Your Kids

No, it's probably too late for you to sign up to get your MBA. The college sites I'm listing are so you can stay knowledgeable about schools for your kids. They're not going to listen to you but if you beat them to the punch and have some ideas on schools and courses, with luck, you can nudge them in the right direction.

www.review.com
This site of the Princeton Review has everything you'll need to know about getting into any college. They even have a separate place for parents to click on.

moneycentral.msn.com/family/home.asp
Tips on saving for college, selecting a college and paying for college. What else do you need to know? Oh yeah, getting the kids in.

www.embark.com
Find, apply to and get your kids into the right school. You can search out any college and apply to leading colleges online.

www.usnews.com/usnews/edu/college/corank.htm
The U.S. News and World Report's annual college rankings. Find out if your old school still makes the grade.

www.universities.com
A data base of 3,000 colleges and universities broken down in many ways and with financial aid information.

www.collegeview.com
Virtual tours of hundreds of colleges. It sure beats driving all over the countryside.

Kids' Camps and Trips

•••❖ **www.camp.ca**
Just type in the kind of camp you think your offspring would be interested in whether it's sailing, riding, computer, cheerleading, gymnastics, foreign or weight loss and so many names will come up that you'll never be able to interview them all. It's unbelievable but there is a camp for every interest.

•••❖ **www.kidscamps.com**
Another directory of camps that offer so many choices your kids will be fighting to go.

•••❖ **www.summercamp.org**
This free public service will give you guidance and referrals for camps worldwide.

•••❖ **www.outwardbound.com**
Teenagers should get excited about these adventure trips. In fact I got pretty excited, and they take parents on some.

•••❖ **www.nols.edu**
National Outdoor Leadership School offers superb leadership and outdoor skill courses in exciting wilderness areas..

Just so you don't feel guilty when you decide on some exotic vacation by yourself, these sites will give you ideas for hundreds of exciting places to send kids that will educate them, broaden their horizons, expand their interests and leave you carefree to enjoy your own time away.

Weddings

Perhaps you are a lucky 50 year old and have a daughter about to get married. We just published a very comprehensive Internet Guide to Weddings and Honeymoons which gives you every bit of information you could possibly want. You can order it from the last page and I've listed a few of the typical sites here.

www.weddingnetwork.com
Tools like wedding planners, local resource guides, online registry, ideas and answers to your questions. You can find everything you need here from "Do Not Disturb" honeymoon signs to planners for managing your guest list.

www.myweddingplans.com
They advertise complete and customized wedding solutions and since they cover everything from dress previews to the top 10 honeymoon sites (plus instructions on how to pack to get there) with etiquette, planning tips, trends and receptions, they just may be correct.

fashionalley.net/wedding.htm
A great site for tips and sources of just about everything.

www.weddingzone.com
Search for your wedding and party services here as well as everything else. The top 50 wedding songs, bridal chat, free wedding planning software and much more.

www.honeymoonislands.com
Honeymoon packages for all the favorite sites; Mexico, Hawaii, South Pacific, Caribbean etc.

honeymoons.miningco.com
A very large site that gives you ideas for every possible kind of honeymoon.

Grandmothering

- **www.drtoy.com/drtoy**
  Dr. Toy rates toys and lists the top 100 toys and has links to places you can buy them.

- **www.etoys.com**
  This site certainly makes buying toys easy with an age directory and recommended favorites.

- **imageplaza.com/parenting**
  Great advice on raising children. You'll wish you read this before raising your kids. Now you can advise your children on how to raise your grandchildren. They'll just love you for it.

- **iml.umkc.edu/casww/grandparentsraising.htm**
  Here is a site on grandparents raising their grandchildren and I hope you only need this when you're baby sitting.

- **www.grandparenting.org/Research.htm**
  A long list of articles on grandparenting. You will find something here that applies to you.

Perhaps you married as a teenager and your kids did the same and now you're a young grandmother. Congratulations. They tell me it's one of life's greatest experiences. While I'm not one yet I can dream and at least imagine what sites will be valuable for a grandmother. Perhaps the first thing you will need to learn is current trends in toys. What more can a grandmother do than bring a toy?

Dogs

There should be someone in the family that you can really count on and if, as is likely, you take care of the feeding, your dog is going to be the one. He may protect the house and play with the kids and go for runs with your husband but if you feed old Fido you are the one who'll get licked each time you come home.

www.petnet.com.au/selectapet/dogselectapet.html
Select a dog that matches you and your life style at this site.

www.petnet.com.au/dogs/dogbreedindex.html
Photos and descriptions of most every breed to let you see if you're going to like the dog the computer picked for you.

www.bulldog.org/dogs
Doggy information on the web. Links to specific breeds and all sorts of other information. My God they even cover wolves.

dogs.about.com/pets/dogs
Everything you need to know to care for your dog: grooming, health, housebreaking, food, training, shows plus lots more.

www.petrix.com/dogint
This site ranks the intelligence and obedience of various breeds.

www.akc.org
Lots of help from the American Kennel Club on selecting and buying a pure bred dog.

C ats

www.cfainc.org
The Cat Fanciers Association with information on caring for cats, breeds and colors and the largest registry of pedigreed cats.

www.katsation.com/felinewww
Worldwide feline links with shows, breeds, rescues, pictures and everything.

www.openhere.com/hac/pets/cats
A real web of cat links. One, for example, has about a billion names for cats.

www.fanciers.com
Cat care, breeds, shows, medicine and many, many links to cat shelters and help organizations.

www.best.com/~sirlou/cat.shtml
The history, genetic, gestation, evolution, species chart, information on choosing a cat and anything else you can think of about cats.

Cats are different. They're independent and clean and clever and once you are into them you'll want to fill your house with felines. You've got to resist this urge.

Miscellaneous and Other Stuff

By the time you are 50 you realize that everything can't be exactly categorized. This section has all those things that may interest us but we don't know quite where to put.

www.missinformation.com
An internet advice column for women where you will learn, at least, not to be a virtual internet klutz.

www.getfreestuffdaily.com
I don't know what the downside is but there sure is a lot of free stuff offered here.

hitbox.com
This site claims to rank independent sites, on many subjects, by how many hits they get.

www.babycatalog.com
When you need baby gifts they offer guaranteed low prices.

www.111greetings.com
Send a friend a free electronic greeting card.

www.wtn.ca
You may not know it but women in Canada have their own television network and this is its online site in case you can't get it on your cable.

www.awsda.org
American Women's Self Defense Organization with all the information you need about choosing not to be a victim.

Women's Magazines

www.allthatwomenwant.com
All That Women Want is a British online magazine with all the usual advice, recipes, parenting etc. but with a delightful English flavor.

www.ellemag.com
The online site for Elle, the women's fashion and lifestyle magazine.

www.betterhomesandgardens.com
Food, gardens, homes, health, travel and all the other favorites from the online version of this classic women's magazine.

www.lhj.com/index.shtml
The Ladies Home Journal online with food and health and beauty and shopping.

www.womentodaymagazine.com
An online magazine called Women Today with many features for young women but also lots for us on beauty, lifestyle, money, health and things like that.

thehistorynet.com/WomensHistory
Women's History has articles about the contribution of women in medicine, education, labor, business, and communications. It's fascinating.

healthyliving.women.com/hl
A magazine that promotes a healthy, balanced life style.

goodhousekeeping.women.com/gh/index.htm
Good Housekeeping Magazine gives you online advice on buying smart, eating and staying well, reviews of lots of different products and all the usual.

You probably know most of these magazines and have subscribed to them from time to time but if you want to get their flavor and most of the good advice and not pay a cent you can now find them on the web.

135

Etiquette

www.albion.com/netiquette/book/index.html
Who knew there were so many rules to using the internet? There is a lot to read on this "net etiquette" site and you should read it so you won't be in danger of showing up as a clod.

www.cuisinenet.com/digest/custom/etiquette/manners_intro.shtml
American table manners are tougher than I thought but at least there is a section on what you can eat with your fingers.

hospice-cares.com/hands/library/pt_care/gfriend.html
Some excellent suggestions on bereavement etiquette.

homearts.com/depts/relat/07wedqf1.htm
Wedding etiquette is a much more complicated matter than I realized and this site begins to answer some typical questions. You can send your own questions by email.

www.webofculture.com/refs/gestures.html
Travel etiquette is a minefield and this site gives you tips on proper behavior from Austria to Turkey. Never, for example show the sole of your shoe in Turkey and be sure to keep your wrists on the table in Bulgaria.

www.ci.sat.tx.us/planning/handbook/index.htm
This extensive handbook explains the etiquette of dealing with disabled people.

Astrology

horoscopes.astrology.com
Enjoy a daily dose of destiny. Lots more at this site than just your sign profile and fortunately they're usually general enough so they don't frighten you to death.

horoscopes4u.com
Five hundred links for each Zodiac sign. This site could keep you busy for awhile and if you check each you'd have to give up some other time consuming activities like sleeping, eating and working.

www.astro-horoscopes.com/index1.html
Learn the language of Astrology and explore many frequently asked questions. A large and very comprehensive site.

www.astrola.com/astrolog.html
Learn what a true horoscope involves and why it gives incredibly accurate advice and forecasts.

www.ntic.qc.ca/~rloise/english.html
Tibetan and Chinese Astrology. Much is in French as well as English which gives it an elegant authentic air.

www.astroamerica.com
The Astrology Center of America offers a national clearing house for Astrology books. The list is very extensive and you won't be able to pronounce the names of most of the authors.

You're almost positive that Astrology is bunk but you're never completely sure and it doesn't hurt to check does it? Find out, at least, if this is an auspicious day to shop on the internet.

dult Education

You don't even have to leave your family to go back to school. You can find courses here for independent study and then all you'll have to do is close the door and not care about dinner or the kids fighting.

•••⁝ **www.back2college.com**
An adult and back-to-college site that will link you to online programs as well as colleges offering programs.

•••⁝ **www.womensu.com**
Women's U is a virtual learning community for women, with classes conducted over the telephone.

•••⁝ **www.edupoint.com**
A supersite for adult education allowing you to search 3,000 learning providers with hundreds of thousands of programs from all over the country.

•••⁝ **www.pbs.org/als**
PBS adult learning service which will help you find out about distance learning and locate courses for home study.

•••⁝ **www.suite101.com/welcome.cfm/adult_education**
A good general adult education site with discussions, advice links and information.

•••⁝ **www.edu-marketing.com/AdultEd.htm**
News on adult and distance learning which puts a degree into the reach of everyone, even 50 year old women.

Environmental Concerns

- **www.igc.org/igc/gateway/enindex.html**
  Eco Net will definitely keep you up-to-date on environmental issues with news and discussion forums. They even have a separate women's net.

- **envirolink.org**
  An extensive directory of environmental sites. Don't forget to feed the kids before getting involved in this site.

- **www.ulb.ac.be/ceese/meta/cds.html**
  Best environmental directories and it is very complete and very extensive and surely a lifetime adventure just to check out.

- **www.coopamerica.org/gp**
  The Green Pages online. Search their directory and find out who are the good guys and good products and who the bad.

- **www.ecomall.com/activism/menu.htm**
  Activism alerts so you can get involved with environmental issues with which you are concerned.

- **takeaction.worldwildlife.org**
  The Conservation Action Network is an electronic advocacy network that lets you get information and take action quickly.

If we women don't get involved men will surely destroy the planet and leave a barren wasteland as our legacy for our progeny. So get involved.

Gossip

All the latest juice is here so you don't have to be embarrassed buying the National Enquirer at the check out counter. If you studied the Literature and Art pages carefully you're allowed to have a little fun.

www.gossipcentral.com
Gossip from major newspaper gossip columns and other sources that will keep you on the phone with your friends for hours.

www.jtj.net/jtj/gossip.shtml
This site is about Hollywood gossip but I don't think it's for 50 year olds. There was hardly anything I understood.

entertainment.msn.com/celebs/celebs.asp
If you are into Hollywood gossip this site will be one of your favorites.

www.eonline.com
A busy place that lets you dig through all the latest dirt.

www.suite101.com/welcome.cfm/celebrity_gossip
More celebrity gossip. I think it's time to move on to adult education.

General Women Things

• www.women.com
  Careers and cars to travel and weddings.
  Everything.

• www.state.gov/www/global/women
  International women's issues in various foreign
  countries as related in U.S. Government reports.
  Trafficking in women and girls and the situation in
  Afghanistan among much more.

• www.aware.org
  Effective self defense for intelligent women. This is
  sound advice.

• www.infoxchange.net.au/wise
  An excellent site with lots of links to feminist,
  domestic violence and health information.

• www.joyzine.zip.com.au/feminism/feminism.htm
  A fun Australian weekly online women's magazine.

In case whatever you are interested in wasn't discussed on one of the other pages hopefully it will be covered here.

OTHER GREAT BOOKS BY BOSTON AMERICA

The fine cultivated stores carrying our books really get ticked if you buy direct from the publisher so, if you can, please patronize your local store and let them make a buck. If, however, the fools don't carry a particular title, you can order them from us for $8 postpaid (unless otherwise noted). Credit cards accepted for orders of 3 or more books.

#2700 Rules For Sex On Your Wedding Night
All the rules from undressing the bride to ensuring the groom will respect her in the morning.

#2704 What Every Woman Can Learn From Her Cat You'll learn that an unmade bed is fluffier and there's no problem that can't be helped by a nap among many others.

#2706 Is There Sex After 50?
Everything from swapping for two-25-year olds to finding out it's not sexy tucking your T-shirt into your underpants.

#2707 Beer Is Better Than Women Because...
Beers don't change their minds once you take off their tops and don't expect an hour of foreplay.

#2708 You Know You're Over 30 When...
You start wearing underwear almost all of the time and no longer have to lie on your resume.

#2709 You Know You're Over 40 When...
You feel like the morning after and you can swear you haven't been anywhere and you start to look forward to dull evenings at home.

#2710 You Know You're Over 50 When...
Your arms aren't long enough to hold your reading material and you sit down to put on your underwear.

#2713 Unspeakable Farts
These are the ones that were only whispered about in locker rooms like the "Hold Your Breath Fart" and "The Morning Fart".

#2714 101 Great Drinking Games
A remarkable collection of fun and creative drinking games including all the old favorites and many new ones you can barely imagine.

#2715 How To Have Sex On Your Birthday
Finding a partner, the birthday orgasm, birthday sex games and much more.

#2717 Women Over 40 Are Better Because...
They are smart enough to hire someone to do the cleaning and men at the office actually solicit their advice.

#2718 Women Over 50 Are Better Because...
They don't fall to pieces if you see them without their makeup and are no longer very concerned about being "with it".

#2719 Is There Sex After 40?
Great cartoons analyzing this important subject from sexy cardigans to the bulge that used to be in his trousers.

#2721 Cucumbers Are Better Than Men Because...
They won't make a pass at your friends, don't care if you shave your legs and stay hard for a week.

#2722 Better An Old Fart Than A Young Shithead
A great comparison of the Old Fart who dresses for comfort and the Young Shithead who is afraid of looking like a dork.

#2726 Your New Baby
This is a manual that explains everything from unpacking your new baby to handling kids' plumbing and routine servicing.

#2729 Great Bachelor Parties
This book tells it all from finding a cooperative stripper to getting rid of the father-in-law to damage control with the bride to be.

#2730 Rules For Engaged Couples
Rules for living together, meeting the family, learning to share and planning the wedding.

#2731 The Bachelorette Party
Great pre-party and party ideas and suggestions for everything from limos to outfits to strippers to your behavior in bars.

#2732 Brides Guide To Sex And Marriage
Dealing with your husband's family and learning what he does in the bathroom and secrets of sleeping comfortably together.

#2501 Cowards Guide To Body Piercing
Cartoons and explanations of all the good and horrible places you can put holes in yourself.

Specially priced books:

#1500 Fish Tank Video [$15 postpaid] This fish tank video enables you to experience all the joys of beautiful, colorful and graceful tropical fish without having to care for them. You'll find yourself hypnotized by the delicate beauty of these fish. Approximately 1 hour running time.

#3001 Winning at Strip Poker [$14 postpaid with playing cards] Not only does this book give you tips on winning at poker, but it tells you how to talk beautiful women into playing with you and shows you what they should look like in 96 pages of full color. It also provides a deck of cards with extra aces to help you win.

#3002 Slightly Kinky Sex Games [$10 postpaid] The games include lots of ideas for oils and ice and places and tie ups and should keep a couple's sex life sizzling with imaginative new activities for a year. 96 pages of sexy full color pictures.

#3003 America's Greatest Hooters [$10 postpaid] 96 pages of full color photographs of America's best including the Louisiana Lollipops, New York Knockers, Georgia Peaches, Pennsylvania Pendulums, Minnesota Minis and lots of others.

NEW INTERNET BOOKS!

#2733 Bizarre Internet Sites [$8 postpaid]
Hundreds of unusual and wild internet sites that will shock, disgust and amuse you and take you places you never imagined even existed.

#3100 Kavet's Internet Sites for Your Wedding and Honeymoon [$10 postpaid]
This is a manual that explains everything from unpacking your new baby to handling kids' plumbing and routine servicing.

#3101 Kavet's Internet Sites for Men Over 50 [$10 postpaid] Fifty year olds need all the help they can get and this book gives them almost 1,000 internet sites.

#3102 Kavet's Internet Sites for Women Over 50 [$10 postpaid] This is a manual that explains everything from unpacking your new baby to handling kids' plumbing and routine servicing.

#3104 Kavet's Internet Sites for 40 Year Olds [$10 postpaid] When you are 40 you are busy with a job and kids and houses and cars. This book gives you almost 1,000 internet sites on these and subjects you'd like to make time for like travel, hobbies and sports.

BOSTON AMERICA C*O*R*P

125 Walnut Street, Watertown, MA 02472
tel: (617) 923.1111 • fax: (617) 923.8839